THE EUCHARIST AND
LITURGICAL RENEWAL

The Eucharist
& Liturgical Renewal

ADDRESSES OF THE
LITURGICAL CONFERENCE
*Held in Saint Paul's Church, San Antonio
November 16–18, 1959*

BY

STEPHEN FIELDING BAYNE, JR.

JOHN MARSHALL HOLT

DORA PHYLLIS CHAPLIN

WILFORD OAKLAND CROSS

FRANK STEPHEN CELLIER

ALEXANDER SCHMEMANN

JOHN PARES CRAINE

Foreword By
EVERETT HOLLAND JONES

Edited for The Associated Parishes, Inc.
BY MASSEY HAMILTON SHEPHERD, JR.

NEW YORK   OXFORD UNIVERSITY PRESS
1960

TO THE PARISH OF

SAINT PAUL'S EPISCOPAL CHURCH

SAN ANTONIO

In Commemoration of Its
Seventy-fifth Anniversary

CONTENTS

PREFACE

In these days church men and women are drawn to many conferences concerned with their life and work as Christians. Some of these meetings are necessary to carry on the institutional work of the Church. Others are more largely inspirational, and for this reason doubtless they are all the more needful. Of the latter kind, a few make indelible impress upon the minds and hearts of those who attend. Such indeed was the experience of the seven hundred clergy and laity who came to the Liturgical Conference held November 16–18, 1959, in San Antonio, Texas. To say that this conference was exceptional will need no other demonstration than a reading of the papers there given and herewith published. If a conference can come near to a perfect achievement of its aim, the one in San Antonio may be so described.

The sponsors of the conference were St. Paul's Episcopal Church of San Antonio, observing its seventy-fifth anniversary of parish life, and the clergy and laity of the Associated Parishes, among whom the Rector of St. Paul's, The Reverend James Joseph, has been a charter member and active leader. To his skill and labor in particular, with the generous, zealous, and efficient support of his people, the extraordinary success of this venture was largely due. St. Paul's parish has given a signal testimony to the vitality of a Christian community inspired by the ideals of the Liturgical Movement, and a notable example of how a congregation can make the happy occasion of an anniversary celebration a means of inestimable enrichment to the thought and prayer of the entire Church.

In one sense, the conference in San Antonio was a sequel to the Liturgical Conference held in May 1958 at Grace Church, Madison, Wisconsin, the papers of which are now available under the title *The Liturgical Renewal of the Church* (Oxford University Press, 1960). But the San Antonio addresses are by no means a mere extension of the papers delivered at Madison. They have a unity and consistency all their own—built entirely around the central theme of the meaning of the Eucharist in all its manifold theological, social, and practical implications. There is no other volume that explores the full range and depth of significance of the Church's Eucharistic worship so richly as does this, and provides such an ecumenical dimension for its understanding.

The editor is deeply grateful to all the contributors for their ready help and co-operation in the preparation of their manuscripts for the press. But special mention is due to Dr. Frank Stephen Cellier for many hours spent in assisting editorial work over and beyond the limits of his own notable address.

MASSEY H. SHEPHERD, JR.
*Editor, The Associated
Parishes, Inc.*

February, 1960

FOREWORD

ADDRESS OF WELCOME TO THE LITURGICAL CONFERENCE

By the Right Reverend Everett Holland Jones, D.D., LL.D.

Bishop of West Texas

IN the past few days the editor of one of our national Church magazines told me that he was deeply impressed with the large amount of 'ecclesiastical talent' which was being assembled for the Liturgical Conference in San Antonio, and that he was devoting a large part of one issue to our gathering. I think this is significant evidence of the excellent work that has been done by the Reverend James Joseph and the members of St. Paul's Memorial Church in preparing for this meeting. This conference is one activity in the celebration of the seventy-fifth anniversary of this important parish in our Diocese.

We are impressed by the participants as well as the leaders who are with us tonight. From California and Florida, from Wisconsin and Mexico, you have come for these days of worship and study and discussion. It must mean that we have a deep common concern for the subject before us. We in the Episcopal Church have always felt deeply on the subject of worship—its centrality, its meaning and joy. I rejoice that we are now joining with others to make this great human experience even more meaningful, even more closely related to our life.

I like to think of the Liturgical Movement as a renewed effort to integrate faith, worship, and life into one living whole. I find my own thinking well expressed in the new volume *Viewpoints,* edited by Dean John B. Coburn and Dr. W. N. Pittenger, and published by the Seabury Press:

Every Sunday the services of the Church speak of such things as the renouncing of sin, the living of a new life in Christ, the reception of the Holy Ghost, the sacrificial offering of all things to God. The contemporary liturgical movement challenges Christendom to face the reality of such words. It calls on the Church to celebrate its rites in such a way that the great truths of the gospel will be no longer clothed by a 'dim religious light,' or blurred by the suave monotone of clerical voices, or muffled in archaic formalities. The liturgical movement is not concerned with the sacristan's task of ordering the little details of worship. It is immensely concerned with uttering the 'nowness' of the Cross of the Lord Christ. (page 74.)

If this be our goal and purpose, and if to some extent we achieve this goal, both while we are here and as we return to our homes and parishes, our efforts and planning, our time and our travel, will not have been in vain.

I

THE EUCHARIST AND THE CHURCH

The Right Reverend Stephen Fielding Bayne, Jr.
D.D., S.T.D., LL.D., D.Litt.

*Executive Officer of The Anglican Communion;
Sometime Bishop of Olympia*

THE EUCHARIST AND THE CHURCH

LET me begin with a comment—not necessarily restricted to our Church, for I think it could be made as appropriately of the Reformation tradition as well—that the Anglican Communion has not yet wholly made up its mind about the Eucharist. (No doubt one could equally say that the Roman Catholic Communion is similarly equivocal about the choir offices; but I am talking about us, and not about them.) I am certain all of us would concede a supreme place to the Holy Liturgy, not only in theory but in true devotion as well. Indeed we can say more than that. It is the rare parish nowadays which seeks to be known as a 'Morning Prayer Parish,' or whatever the alternative should be called. Most of our parishes and most of our clergy set out to establish a more central position. Yet even in this blessed centrality, there still is often the sense that there is a choice to be made. Our centrality consists in offering a more equal choice than was once true. There is always an opportunity, even in the most Matins-minded congregation, for what may be somewhat sniffily referred to as 'an early Communion,' and Morning Prayer is usually tucked in somewhere even in the most Eucharistically-minded congregation. But it is still clearly a matter of choice. I am sorry that it is so, and I pray most sincerely for the day when no such choice shall ever be forced on Church men and women. Yet I know that it is so forced.

And inevitably people take sides. Sometimes they take sides for quite foolish reasons. There are the historically foolish-minded who choose Morning Prayer on the general basis that what was good enough for George Washington is good enough for them, or alternatively choose the Holy Communion under the somewhat fond delusion that St. Paul was generally to be found with his finger inserted at page 67 in the Prayer Book. There are the ceremonially foolish people, who choose Matins because they like the apostolic, black-and-white austerity of surplice and scarf, or alternatively prefer the other because of the slightly antique and Mediterranean flavor the appropriate garments communicate to worship.

The god of Morning Prayer sometimes seems a more manageable deity to people. Morning Prayer offers little scope for sacerdotal monkeyshines. It is a sober, reasonable approach to a sober, reasonable god, by which a well-intentioned and somewhat Pelagian gentleman can approach Him. Or contrarywise, the god of the sacraments seems more 'real,' as we say. Theory is too much with us, and there is a clearer sense of the supernatural about sacramental worship, no matter whether one really believes in the god or not. Like the mildly acid comment about a great Harvard philosopher, that for him 'there is no god, and Mary is his mother,' our generation is sometimes drawn to a somewhat parallel substitution of horsepower for reason.

These are all unworthy rationalizations, of course, and we all know it. Yet the problem of the choice between the choir offices and the Eucharist is a real problem; and I am quite certain that I am right in saying that we of the Anglican tradition have not yet wholly made up our minds about the choice. And I must confess that I have some sympathy with this equivocal state of mind. Our Eucharistic liturgy suffers by comparison with Morning Prayer, in the thought and experience of many very sincere people. At least superficially, our liturgy is not a dynamic, congregational experience, and Morning Prayer is. There is far too much monologue about the Eucharist. It lacks the somewhat athletic participation of the choir offices. It encourages a 'cafeteria spirituality' which nourishes loneliness rather than breaking down the 'middle wall of partition.' It is also infected with clericalism to a distressing degree, in the experience of many ordinary churchmen who, like most others of the clergy and laity, suffer from a chronic case of anti-clericalism. For still another thing, preaching is much harder to do (for me at any rate) in the context of the liturgy, than it is in the context of the choir offices. (I think the reason for this, as far as I can understand my own technique of preaching at any rate, is that the dialogue and conversation within the framework of Morning Prayer helps create a congregation—helps bring the congregation into existence—in a way in which the rather prosy monologue of the Eucharist does not. But this may be only an eccentricity of my own.)

How seriously one ought to take any of these factors is a matter of opinion. My point here is only this—that in the cases of a distressing number of churchmen a choice must somehow be made; that the choice is often for very foolish reasons; and that there are also some very thought-provoking reasons expressed in the choices made. The things I have mentioned at any rate make me long for the day when liturgical knowledge and liturgical skill can help guide the Church to the point where no choice need be made. God speed that day—the day when we have recovered within the Eucharistic liturgy the whole-hearted congregational dialogue and participation it ought to have; when we have brought those second cousins, the pro-Anaphora and the choir offices, together again, so that there is a fully Biblical preparation for the Eucharistic acts, which will contain all of the quiet gravity of Morning Prayer, and all its deep sense of God's action in history and His moral demands on us.

Yet, even assuming the greatest liturgical knowledge and skill, we should still have one massive central problem to face. People will still be hankering for the choice of Morning Prayer until the end of time unless we can somehow capture a clear sense of the glorious, terrible relevance of the liturgy. The Blessed Sacrament is, for a tragically great number of people, an unrelated mystery. It is a tale told of something that happened long ago; it is a barren parable of what men dream might some day happen; it is a mysterious priestly transaction—it is the *unrelated mystery* of the Eucharist which creates the problem. Therefore if any man is going to speak about the Eucharist and the Church, he must of necessity speak of its *meaning*, within the life of the Church and within the life of the churchman.

We have all had our tries at this. Sometimes we have approached the problem by concentrating on the acted parable of the Eucharist. We have fixed our eyes on the action and have sought to relate the action step by step with our own condition. Nobody will deny that this is an essential step in understanding the liturgy. We cannot understand the Eucharist at all unless we can see clearly the great acts of offering and sacrifice and thanksgiving and communion, and make them our own. But this alone is not enough; this alone might be no more than the thin little parable of brotherhood and love which is all that many people now see in the Eucharist. And this is not enough. Christ did not break the bread and die on the Cross in order to provide some milk-and-water play-acting for amiable people. There is a being and a mystery here; and to fail to sense that being and mystery is to fail to understand the very heart of historic sacramental Christianity. It is also to fail to do justice to some of man-

kind's deepest impulses. No theology is going to be very true
or get very far which short-changes man by refusing to tackle
the thing that lies at the very heart of his quest. What mankind seeks in the liturgy is not a reflection of our needs or our
impulses, even the best of them. What we are seeking is the
action of God.

Sometimes the words—the Eucharistic words—offer an inviting challenge to thought and interpretation. Of them all,
perhaps the chief is the word 'sacrifice.' In a culture like
ours, sacrifice can have no clear meaning. If we use it at all,
we are likely to use it almost exclusively as part of the slang
of the Every Member Canvass. I do not scorn 'sacrificial giving,' when it is worthy of the name. Yet how dismally often
we mean by the word 'sacrifice' no more than a passing dis-
comfort. And to a people accustomed to using 'sacrifice' to
refer to an additional half dollar a week, the same word applied to the mystery of the Cross and of the Altar is almost
ludicrous. We do not understand that it is a word about
death; we understand even less that it is a word about the
release of life through death. To the man of the world, the
thought of how it could be that life could pour itself out
through death is a ridiculous thought. It is part of the 'holy
language' which the Church keeps using, which he wishes the
Church would somehow modernize.

All this offers a most inviting opportunity for fresh translation. It may well be that a new pathway to relevance and
meaning will be found when we can somehow recapture the
word 'sacrifice' (or an equivalent, if there be one), and the
fact of sacrifice, and reflect on how immense an act a sacrifice
must be and on how great its implications are. The freedom
which is expressed in the choice of the Victim, the death of
the Victim itself, the rush of life through that death to be
communicated to those who share in the sacrifice, the neces-

sary participation in the sacrifice which alone makes it meaningful for those who are to share it—all these cry aloud for
re-examination. And it may well be that in due course we
may come to that examination.

Until that time, a clear division is bound to exist in the
Church's life—a division between those to whom the word and
idea of sacrifice are meaningful, and those to whom the word
is merely an antique piety and nothing more.

I suspect that the deepest division of all, in this sacramental
life of ours, is the wrestling within the soul of the Church—
like Jacob and Esau in Rebekah's womb—between the two,
great, possible ways of understanding and saying what
Christ's offering of Himself did for us and must mean for us.

To one spirit in the Church, the great weight must fall on
the dimension of Time. The supreme offering on Calvary—
this wonderful, free-giving of Himself by Himself—this is a
once-for-all event. Never again could this happen; never
again need it happen. We who come after remember that
sacrifice; we enter into our inheritance from Him whom we
remember. With humble thanksgiving we do what He did
and say what He said, obedient to His commandment, for the
recalling of what was done for us once for all.

Having in remembrance, as our Prayer Book says, how He
'made there (by his one oblation of himself once offered) a
full, perfect, and sufficient sacrifice, oblation, and satisfaction,' we keep this perpetual and obedient memorial, until
His coming again. Thus, Time is in our heart's blood; we
can no more escape it than we can escape the need to breathe.
All reality can only be known by us when it is stretched out,
mounted, framed in the framework of Time.

This supreme fact of Calvary, on which our whole religion
is built, this is to be taken seriously, as a fact of history. It
was no symbolic ritual, nor a pageant to be displayed again

and again. It is in deadly earnest. It happened once, for only
once can such an offering by such a High Priest be made.

So pleads one spirit within the Church. The Reformation
Christians knew that spirit well, but it was no exclusive prop-
erty of the Reformers. They spoke for a continuing spirit
which has never been lacking in Christian thought and
devotion. It is the spirit which has always nourished within
Christian faith the sturdy, humbling sense of history. We
did not invent the gospel. Man did not write the Christian
faith to suit his own time and condition. God did these things;
and our part is to abide obediently by what He did, and by
the faithfulness of our recalling to establish our companion-
ship with Him over all the years.

All well and good—all true—responds the other spirit, but
adds quite rightly that what we are remembering is not only
the event in Time. It is also an eternal truth about God. The
Lord Jesus is not dead. Our memorial is something infinitely
more than merely to remember Him who lived a long time
ago. What we remember is the moment when God Himself
entered into Time, and showed us what His love was really
like. Therefore the greater weight must fall on God's action
and God's being, not on our remembrance. *The sacrifice
is an eternal fact about God.* The Eucharist can only be understood in terms of an eternal offering, which indeed may
be re-presented or re-enacted on every altar, every day, but
which is, first of all, outside Time altogether.

Who will deny the truth of this? Probably in the liturgies
of the Orthodox Churches this sense of the eternal fact of the
offering rises to its highest degree—this wonderful, timeless,
mystic sense of the eternal action of God, of the love which
is unchangingly and unfailingly true about Him who reigns
beyond the veil of time and space. Yet all true Christian
devotion everywhere knows something of this sense, which

gives us that precious assurance of the objective reality of God's action and presence in the Blessed Sacrament. The Eucharist is a work done by God, we say. It does not depend on the worthiness of the minister or the depth or moral sincerity of the worshipper's acceptance of his heritage. Serene and fixed above all the changes and chances of this mortal life and our human, moral failure, God the Son makes His immortal, free offering of Himself to the eternal Father.

I have tried to sketch two spirits—in theology and devotion alike—both of which have their proper place in Christian life. The Church tends to move from one to the other; indeed we do ourselves as individuals. Ideally we should doubtless feel that both were equally our birthright. But it has not happened that way in Christian history.

The spirits have become hostile, unreconciled. We have felt that we had to choose between them. That gigantic earthquake, the Reformation, opened great schisms between Christians and between our churches; and all too often the line of division was a frontier between these two spirits. Men to whom the action of God in Time was most precious and meaningful looked with suspicion at the devotion and life of others nurtured in the sense of Eternity. 'Your sacrament is nothing but magic,' they said, 'it costs you nothing; it asks nothing of your moral earnestness.' And then from the other side came equally harsh charges: 'You make of the Eucharist a purely subjective commemoration. All depends on you and your sincerity. You act as if Jesus were a good, dead man whose only ministry now is in the effectiveness of your recalling of Him.'

Who has not heard such judgments, or perhaps even shared in them? How have they not separated Christians one from another? Even within the same Church, the same charges may be heard—'Magic . . . superstition,' or else

'Merely a memorial.' And there is enough truth to sting, on both sides. How arid and sterile the devotion of the later Middle Ages became, for example, when fewer and fewer Christians shared in the liturgy, when the Eucharist was something to be seen and wondered at, not something to be shared and received! Our hymns, our theology, became a barren celebration of a philosophical system: transubstantiation. 'How does God do this?' became the question for devotion, not 'How great is His love for me; how much then must I love the brethren!'

On the other side, how shabby and shallow does our devotion become when the dimension of Eternity is lost! So intent and preoccupied do we grow in the search for the grace to re-create a pure and moving memory of what Jesus did, that we lose, little by little, any sense of the unceasing, eternal work of God for us. It all seems to depend on us; and our remembrance of Christ dwindles until it is no more than a tantalizing memory of a perfect man, long ago, whose spirit we invoke when we share this common meal. On one side, we exalt and multiply the Eucharist as our ritual act, at the cost of losing all sense of our responsible participation in it. On the other, we come less and less frequently to celebrate it, aware of our own failure to reach the perfect remembrance we seek, and increasingly mystified as to the necessity of any such liturgical act at all.

Am I exaggerating? Of course. There are no such pure spirits; and no man is entirely of one opinion or the other. Yet the fact is that the Eucharist, which was given of Christ to be our center of unity, has become the no-man's-land, the frontier of our disunity. Here, where we should be together, we are most apart. The reasons are not only (I should say not even primarily) reasons of order and authority. They are far deeper reasons, in the suspicions and misunderstandings of men who feel that they must somehow choose between two exclusive interpretations—men who do choose (or grow up in their fathers' choices), and to whom the devotion and faith of each is closed and suspect to the other and somehow dark and unworthy.

Because the very unity of Christ's Body is at stake in this, it is much more than simply an interesting philosophical contrast. Of course, it is the age-old problem of Time and Eternity—the mind of man has wrestled with it ever since we began to think at all. But so is Jesus Christ a problem in Time and Eternity, and nobody will shrug Him off as an interesting exercise in speculative theology! Our loyalty to Christ, our unity in Him, the utter, devastating importance of His cause in this divided world—these are matters of critical and urgent importance, not of passing philosophical curiosity. And of equal gravity must be the question of our unity in the one great service which He commanded us to do together.

Must we choose between these two ways of thinking? Are they exclusive of each other? I think our Anglican answer would be No. If our religion had to be contained within one single, exclusive philosophical system, then we might be caught in this dilemma. For then we should have to choose between one set of categories and another. We should have to fit our prayers and our choices either into the framework of the classic, Greek words and ideas, and take as our central problem the way in which eternal reality can be made even partially real in Time, or else choose another framework, perhaps the mainly Biblical one of history, and then worry about whatever ghostlike reality Eternity can have when it is disembodied of Time.

The intellectual tragedy of Western Christianity has been precisely here, for the most part, in being made captive of the philosophies it has created. How often Catholic theology, after the Reformation at any rate, deliberately imprisoned itself inside the formal categories of Aristotle's thought; and even the noblest bondage in the most spacious and lofty of prisons is imprisonment still. We need not wonder why so much modern Eucharistic devotion has the air of nostalgic poetry scratched on the walls of a cell.

But 'sterile' is the word for much Protestant devotion, too— a barren crunching on the bones left over from the medieval feast, as if there were nothing still to be learned, nor any century that mattered except the first and the sixteenth. *Philosophy serves Faith*—not the other way around. The facts of God's action in history—these are the primary data of philosophy. And a living faith will squeeze what juice it likes out of any philosophy, and then encourage new ones in their turn.

The fact is that God, in Christ, made the supreme offering for us, once and once only (as we count 'once'). This is an event in history, for the Incarnation is real, and the freedom of Christ is real, and His manhood is real. He chose, once, to be both Priest and Victim, for His obedience and His freedom alike required it. Once, Man did this; and ever after this unique sacrifice remains a pinnacle in human history.

It is also a fact about God. This is the supreme revelation of what God's love is like. For both sides of the Incarnation are real. It was the Word of God who was made flesh; and what the Word did on earth is our surest knowledge of what is eternally true about God. God so loved the world that once He sent His only-begotten Son; God so loves the world that that coming-once-for-all is the revelation of what God eternally and unchangeably is and does.

We learn over and over again how we must hold those two sides of the Incarnation together. Christ is not merely man, nor is His manhood simply a puppet which God manipulates behind the scenes. Very God and very man—such is the un-changing response of faith whenever we ask the question, 'Is Christ God or is He man?' The fullness of the Godhead—never failing, never changing—yet is expressed in the brief, ever changing, mortal life of a man.

And this is exactly the response we make to the dilemma of Time and Eternity in the Eucharist. What God eternally does and is can be known to us only in His successive acts in history. Yet the things which happen in history are themselves meaningless until they carry us to the eternal God who does them. If the love of God is real, then we shall see in them tiny sparkles of the immortal fire of His unchanging love.

If Time has no reality—if the Act of God need not, or can-not, be fulfilled in Time and time-bound souls—then neither Passion nor Eucharist is more than a pale myth, and all of human struggle and freedom is a ridiculous and pitiful illu-sion. If Eternity is no more than an abstraction, and Time is all we know, then the Act of God is no more than the elongated shadow of hopes and dreams, which has no more reality than they do. Time and Eternity *must* meet, in our limited human experience, if there is to be substance in the choices we must make or in the thoughts by which, willy-nilly, we must live. And the Passion and the Eucharist are the supreme meeting-place.

If the Son of God died for us on Calvary, then He died for every one, all of the living, all of the dead, all of those still to come. He died once; yet He must die for everyone of the brotherhood, and in us all, for 'He must reign, till he hath put all enemies under his feet.' God's love is not love of an abstraction or an ideal; it is a love for particular human souls, for *us,* for the likes of us, for the multitude who are born into freedom and must learn at bitter cost how to bear it like true men. Therefore God's love must needs be actualized, made real, in the soul of every one of His children.

God is patient with Time. He created it; He made us creatures of it; then He is content to abide the condition of our creation, for His love's sake, and pay the cost of it in the tireless re-enactment of His redeeming sacrifice in the soul of every stubborn, lonely, human fragment.

But so must we then accept this love, time and time again, and let Christ's offering be made real in our wills. It is only half the truth to say that God in Christ made the perfect offering. The offering cannot be completed until it is as real as Time is, with whatever reality Time has. It cannot be completed until 'we offer and present ourselves, our souls and bodies, to be a reasonable, holy, and living sacrifice' to the Father, through and in and with the Son, who is our Brother. To unite ourselves with the great act of God's love in Christ—to let our Lord reproduce Himself, His life, His free offering, in each of us—to fulfill in our daily lives the perfect manhood which He first showed to us—these are the Eucharistic imperatives, equally with the assurance that Christ is the eternal Priest who made the offering once for all for us.

If this were not so, then what would the Eucharist be save some gigantic parlor-trick which amazes and stupifies us, but with which we have no relation save that of spectator? Time and Eternity must ever be held together, and the meeting-place is in the soul of mankind; and it is at the altar. And until our tiny, daily sacrifices of self are brought to the altar to be joined to His universal sacrifice, and His offering fulfilled in our offering, the work of Christ is not done. It was for Him alone to have the superb freedom to make the offering once for all. We do not have that freedom. Divided and fragmented as we are, we are lucky if we can offer Him one hour. Even Peter and James and John could not offer Him one hour. Yet patiently He waits and works within us, constrained by His love and His pity for free and time-bound creatures; and day by day we bring a little more of ourselves to the altar and put our little fraction of freedom into His hands and say, 'Lord, accept this offering, and add it to Thine own.' And He does. And day by day He moves through our lives— leading, guarding, warning, strengthening—doing all that a Christ-like God could do to fulfill His love in us.

What does St. Paul say? We must be 'always bearing about in the body the dying of the Lord Jesus, that the life also of Jesus may be made manifest in our body.' This is the mark of the Christian life, this daily, public witness in our lives to His sacrificial love: the 'dying of the Lord Jesus.' He must die in us, through our daily death to sin and to the imprisonment of this world. Yet, as with Him, the dying is the gateway to life. We die, in our daily, disciplined offering of ourselves; yet the dying is only the preface to the gift of life which He makes to us and in us.

Do you doubt this? Have you never wrestled with temptation, and by God's grace let go of it finally and given it up to Him—died to it, and not found the sudden surge of strength which comes to you to take its place? Have you never chosen the hard, Christian witness, and died to all the other, comfortable possibilities of life, and not felt His serenity and grace sweep over you?

Do not ask where or when the sacrifice of Calvary is made. It was made once, two thousand years ago; yet it is made, by Christ, in us, every time we offer ourselves to Him. The Eucharist is not a Church service, it is a way of life; just as Calvary was not an unfortunate close to a beautiful interlude, but the controlling pattern of Christ's whole ministry to us.

We do not learn anything new about Christ at Calvary. We knew all this before—His love, His royal freedom, His obedience, His marvelous self-offering. All this we knew from Jordan and the Wilderness. Calvary sums up, in a single, final act what is always true about Jesus, what is always true about God, what is God's idea of what it is to be a man.

So then, Calvary must become the daily pattern for the disciple. And the Eucharist is Calvary. It is the taking and the breaking and the giving of His life, world without end, by us, in us, with Him, in Him, until the dying of the Lord Jesus in the lives of all His flock is accomplished, and His life reigns unchallenged and serene.

What I am really saying is that there is an inescapable continuity, even an identity, between Calvary and the Church and the Christian within the Church; and that the Eucharist is the vessel and means of that identity, the act which establishes the bridge between Eternity and Time, and makes 'identity' the right word. Calvary is the whole of the life and love of the Lord Jesus gathered into one awful moment. The Church is the life of Calvary, the life of the Lord, extended out through Time. The Christian's life is the pattern of Calvary, acted out by Christ in us, choice after choice, day after day, act by act. And always it is the Eucharist which binds and holds all this together in Time and out of Time. The Church is the eucharistic Body, and Christians are the eucharistic people, the people who take their lives, and break them, and give them, in daily fulfillment of what our Lord did and does. No need to ask what school of thought you follow or how you speculate about the manner of these things. He took His life in His own hands—this is freedom. He broke it—this is obedience. He gave it—this is love. And He still does these simple acts at every altar and in every heart that will have it so. And Time and Eternity meet. The dying of the Lord Jesus and His life weave the wonderful humble fabric of Christian discipleship.

If God did not love us so much, then He would not wait for us to let Him fulfill His will in us. The waiting until Calvary is fulfilled and complete in every soul—the waiting is part of the pain of Calvary. If God did not remember that He made us so, and patiently accept the condition of our mortality, then His offering might indeed have been made once and once alone, and we be abandoned in the loneliness of a fruitless memory. But Time is God's gift as well as our condition. He has bound Himself by it in our making, and so also in our redeeming. Therefore there is a meeting between Time and Eternity, for His love's sake. And that meeting is in our wills.

To make our hearts an altar, to make our bodies bread good enough for His hands, to ask no more of our discipleship than that we may offer ourselves to Him and in Him, to look at our life and see in it the stuff of His great offering even as our wheat and grapes become the sacramental bread and wine of the liturgy, to perceive Him as the great High Priest who forms us and acts in us in proportion as we are prepared to let Him act—these are the marks of the eucharistic people, and they are the marks of the eucharistic Church.

You do not choose between Eternity and Time. You do not choose to remember. These are the false choices which divided us in holy things. The truth is that there is no Time which is not caught up into Eternity, and no Eternity which must not make itself real in Time. There is one offering and one sacrifice, never to be repeated, which yet must be worked out in the hearts and wills of every prisoner of Time. The dying of the Lord Jesus in our bodies—this is the unity of the altar; this is the essential nature of the Church.

For the mysticism of the Eucharist is not a mysticism of

metaphysics. It is a mysticism of the will. The identifying of
our separate manhood, our free and individual and stubborn
personalities, with His perfect manhood in His perfect offering, this is not to be done in spite of our selfhood or by obliter-
ating our selfhood. It will be done in the Eucharist's own way,
by the obedience with which, remembering His offering in
Time, the Church yields itself freely to it, asking only that by
the dying of the Lord Jesus in us, He may live in us and make
us one with Him and one with one another in Him. Our
selves then, in their true freedom, by our own choice and His
redeeming grace, will be the true selves God created them
to be, and all shall be one in God's own way and in His own
time.

Have I said now what I wanted to say?—that the choice
between the choir offices and the Eucharist is still with us in
Anglican life; that it is a choice often made for silly reasons,
but not always; that the liturgical scholars can do a great
service for us in bringing together again the Biblical offices
and the pro-Anaphora; that that union alone cannot end the
equivocation in Anglicanism or the schism which produces it;
that nothing can finally end that schism except a whole-
hearted recovery of the sense of moral earnestness and profound personal and social responsibility, which is really at
the heart of the Eucharist, but so often does not appear?

It is no wonder that sober and earnest people so often turn
to the Biblical emphasis of Morning Prayer and its overtones
of moral responsibility. For many of them the Eucharist,
with all its splendid beauty, is an unrelated mystery, a memory without consequence, a dream from which one must
wake to the more responsible world of daily life.

We who care, as I care with all my heart, that this schism
should end, and that the Eucharist, restored and full with
every note and impulse of moral seriousness, should be the

universal pattern of the Church's worship and its life—we have a task yet to do. It is the task of recovering the unity of Calvary and Church and Eucharist, of seeing and proclaiming the patience of God who waits for His love to be fulfilled in every man's will, who waits and bears the eternal pain of the Cross until the true nature of our manhood is worked out in every man's life.

The Eucharist is no incidental devotion, added to strengthen our responsible freedom. It is the focus of that responsibility, and the summit of that freedom. It is the form of the death of Christ (and therefore His life—and therefore of the Church's life and its continual death—and therefore of the death and life and the life-in-death of every Christian). The Eucharist is the present form of the Act of God, in Time, and the supreme Act of God, which yet will not be supreme until it is acted out in the lives of those for whom God waits, in terrible and costly patience. Therefore, my brethren, it behooves us to hasten, that the form of Calvary may be the form of the Church, that the altar may be the means and the mold of our daily lives, that Christ may dwell in us and we in Him.

II

THE EUCHARIST AND THE BIBLE

The Reverend John Marshall Holt, Ph.D.

Associate Professor of Hebrew and Old Testament,
The Episcopal Theological Seminary of the Southwest

THE EUCHARIST AND THE BIBLE

THE Christian lives his life in response to grace, receiving redemption and replying to that love with the appropriate surrender of heart, mind, and soul. The character of the grace is such that he can do no other; the redemption is such that nothing but the dedication of his whole life to responding to it will do. Even that is inadequate, in the final evaluation of things, but it is the most that the Christian can do as a man. —This is the long and short of life as the Christian sees it, and any attempt to discuss any aspect of the Christian life of worship, study, or action in the world against any other background is doomed to theological shallowness and inadequacy. Thus, to approach, as I have been assigned, the consideration of the Eucharist and the Bible, their relationship and kinship to each other in the Christian's worshipping and living, requires that we see Eucharistic action and Biblical record of revelation as themselves fitting into this essential pattern of life as the Christian sees it.

It is the faith of Christian people, amidst all the varieties of Christian explanation or avoidance of explanation of it, that in the faithful performance of the Eucharistic liturgy— no matter how nonliturgical it sometimes becomes and no matter how obscure the strictly Eucharistic element in it may be here and there—they nevertheless are the recipients of a gift which only God in Christ can give and which he lovingly does give them: participation in his own life and glory. It is grace, an application of redemption to their sinful lives surrendered in worship, which calls for the response of obedience to the will of the Lord who thus shares the gift with them. Likewise, within all the range of possible opinion about the literalness with which the authenticity of Scripture is to be considered 'inspired' and about the degree of superiority and continuity between Old and New Covenants, it is nevertheless the conviction of Christian people that in the received Scripture of the Old and New Testaments there are laid out a credible account of the most significant segment of the world's history and, what is more, the most significant interpretation of that account, so that the Scriptures truly stand to the Christian as the record of revelation, the story of redemption, the history of salvation. It is God's challenge to man to see and believe the Lordship of his God in action. It is, again, confrontation with redemption that demands response.

Furthermore, neither Scriptural record nor Eucharistic worship can be properly studied or appropriated into Christian living without their being seen as, in both cases, instances of this human response raised up by the divine initiative and accompanying it. They are both confrontation and response. Many unwholesome doctrines of the Eucharist have resulted from overattentiveness to what it is that God is doing in His initiative there, just as dreadful distortions of the Bible have resulted from our eagerness to assert the human agency which produced it. In each of these, its converse is true, and the decision to phrase them just this way is not argumentatively significant; it could just as easily have been the other way around. What does count is the insistence that we shall never see either Eucharist or Bible in full depth without recognizing in both the divine initiative and its use of the co-operating human agency, responding to the gift of redemption. This is the main matter of the Incarnation itself, and it is the central content of the answer to the question, 'What is going on here?' In Bible and Eucharist, in the guide to life and its interpretation which the Scriptures provide with their evaluated account of God's mighty acts, and in that focal action which is the mainstay of the Christian life lived according to that guidance, what is 'going on here' is that man is receiving redemption, a congregation is being met by their Saviour: humanity is being taken into responsive fellowship with God.

How strange this language sounds in this crazy world of the second half of the twentieth century! What a fantastic answer to the question conceivably put to us by the outside world, if they bother to notice at all what we are about and ask for its meaning! For, after all, this is on a totally different level of speaking; this is a different kind of interpretation of life from that to which the world outside the Church is accustomed. Services in the Church, whether the Eucharist or some other? Why, as the world sees these things, these are part of the leisure-time activities of that segment of the population who still manage to maintain an interest in this esoteric kind of pious activity off to one side of life, although the life of society as a whole during the past one hundred and fifty years has seen the gradual disappearance of the once universally expected and accepted fact of church membership. This is what the world of the twentieth century thinks of the Eucharistic action and its satellite offices.

And the Bible? How little understanding of its real meaning to Christian people can be found in this age! In a time when everybody talks about the Bible's being the top bestseller in the book market, not only can a sizable number of men on the street not name or summarize the main content of more than two or three of its component books, but far too many of those who claim to follow its rule of living cannot decide whether it is to be viewed as an interesting remnant of an ancient body of literature translated into a splendid specimen of the English language at its most vigorously expressive, or as an almanac and oracle filled with arcane lore which is to be tricked out of its concealment by the clever discovery of its tantalizingly half-hidden key. In either case, the Bible is to this age a largely irrelevant and noncommunicating assemblage of whatever type of literature it may be, with as little import for life as it is actually lived as the strange actions of the Eucharist.

This is what it all looks like to the people outside, and at this point, what Christian people need to learn to be able to communicate is not only that Eucharistic action and Scriptural tradition both have significance far beyond their outward appearance, but also that the same basic significance and function give meaning to both: confrontation with redemption and response to grace. It is, of course, true that Eucharist and Scripture have this significance and function for Christian people by virtue of the faith in which the people of the Church receive and do them. This is, however, to say only what we acknowledge on all sides: that the ultimate perception of the Christian mysteries demands that the inquirer share the faith of Christians themselves.

Man's response to God's grace can be classified and categorized variously, but for the purposes of this study the response can be most conveniently considered in these three aspects: the cultic, the theological, and the ethical. We here encounter the danger of overlapping terms in our language, just as we run up against that of leaving some aspects of life untouched by any of our categories; but we run the same risks even when we speak of man's response as loving the Lord his God with all his heart and with all his soul and with all his mind and with all his strength. Any attempt, Biblical or other, to divide or parcel off an ultimately indivisible thing like the total response of a human life will meet the same fate. The division is a useful one, though, for in these three great areas of life can be helpfully seen how Eucharist and Bible, alike in their respective functions, participate in a common importance which is not a reductionist oversimplification but a recognition of congruent unity. This is the principal and inclusive statement this paper has to make.

Each of these three in its Godward aspect, the cultic, the theological, and the ethical, is an offering of life in response to received redemption: redemption received, accepted, and personally appropriated. The cultic is the obvious one that comes to mind when one thinks of what people ordinarily call 'religious.' In this cult with its signs, its symbols, and its ceremonies the story of salvation is rehearsed and relived so that the cult and its functionaries serve as the memory of the redeemed people. It spans the time between the great past event and the pressing present moment so as to remember the past, not as something gone and only recalled, but as demandingly present and relevant to the present time. Cult recites tradition so as to experience it anew and thereby achieve an equidistance from the historic event of redemption for all subsequent points in time. The past becomes present and experienceable in its cultic re-enactment and representation.

Theology is similarly an offering of life in response to grace, for here is the application of man's intellectual capacity, by which he orders his life as a whole, to this experience of redemption. The discipline of the mind, by which a man asks himself what he is doing and what his life means, goes to work on what cultic memory recaptures and asks it the penetrating questions whose answers serve to draw out the meaning and import of the experience. It is a sad fact of our life in this anti-intellectual stage of our history in this country that this aspect of the response to grace has to fight for recognition as what it is, as against the notion of theology as the impediment to the service of God which mean-minded men hold it to be. The truth of it is that the theological aspect of man's response to redemption serves to protect the whole process of response from degeneration into barren dumbshow or vicious superstition by recognizing the experience of salvation as something which commands the attention of man's highest and best faculty and its interpretive ability.

As for the ethical, it is one of the glories of Biblical religion that it insists that true religion must always be more than just the strictly 'religious' and must issue forth in concrete behavior. With the historic unconcern of the Hebrew mind for the speculative and abstract and the constant prophetic reminder of the inadequacy of anything but man's penitence as a substitute for absolute righteousness, Biblical ethics as a whole demands upright and good living in those who have experienced redemption, and for that reason supremely that they have experienced redemption. There are the prudential considerations of enlightened, even calculating self-interest in Biblical ethical statements, to be sure, but the dominating theme throughout is nevertheless that those who have received salvation must live lives expressing gratitude for it. Here lies the essence of the Bible's unique demand for something more than either cultic or moral formalism, for total dedication of life to the redeemer; and thus ethics seeks to draw out of the experience of redemption the principles and patterns of its implications for people's behavior.

The redeemed, then, enter anew into the events of their salvation in the cult; they consider the meaning of the events in their theological thought; and their ethical statements show them how to live as befits those who have been so confronted. Each of these three categories as directed toward God offers the responding life of the redeemed in fidelity and surrender. In the manward aspect of these categories, likewise, each has a specific function to perform. Cult, theology, and ethics do things to men just as they offer something to God.

The cultic serves as the covenanted meeting-place of the redeemer and the redeemed, so that the latter, experiencing afresh the act of the redeemer, finds himself confirmed and established in his conviction that truly God has laid His hand on him. He knows this has happened to him because he has experienced it himself. It would be a ghastly perversion of things to think of the cultic action as existing only to inspire and uplift the worshipper's sagging heart, but that is not what we are saying here. Here we simply consider the fact that cultic experience serves as the locus of the deepening and fortification of the worshipper's faith through the best of all possible methods, his own direct, personal penetration into and appropriation of the act of the author and finisher of that faith.

In the same way theology in its manward aspect does man the great service of giving him, at each step in its on-going process of questioning, the presently available working answers to the deepest problems of life. These are not the answers to the petty or frantic questionings of mischief or unfaith, nor are they the pompous pronouncements of dogmatism; for, when theology is really doing its business, it always points out areas as yet unexplored and unconsidered. Theology, considered as acting toward man, gives him the growing interpretation of the meaning of his redeemer, his redemption, and his own redeemed self in terms of his existing situation where he is.

Again, it is quite apparent in the case of ethics what its achievement for man is. We must constantly be reminded of the distance between where we and our society are and where we ought to be. It is the peculiar task of our ethical concern to confront us again and again with this disparity and incongruity. If we are to act as those who have been redeemed, then our efforts must be directed toward the yet unfulfilled standards and goals which ethics sets before us.

This, as a matter of fact, brings the subject to a helpful point: the same cult, theology, and ethics which serve as the main categories for our Godward response to redemption are likewise lights and guides for our living. The same process acts in both directions, toward God and man, at once. It would be untrue to the Bible's best light to view this process of redemption as something done entirely by a loving God who only poured it from above into a patient receptacle below, just as it would be to see in it nothing more than man's heroic struggle from below in search of God. The work of redemption proceeds from the initial divine impetus which alone can give it ultimate validity, and because it involves persons with the capacity for self-determination and operates on the principle of unforced love, it calls for and provides for the participation of the recipient in its achievement: the momentum is simultaneously Godward and manward, as the Bible's most mature thought sees it.

There is more to be said about the categories of the response to redemption than that they operate in both directions between God and man. Since we are considering the Holy Scriptures and the Eucharistic action as two functions of this process, it is equally important for us to note that not a one of the categories of the response can stand by itself. To try to make any of them do so is to fall into that atrocious distortion of truth which can result only when part of it is taken as the whole, that awful impoverishment for which we reserve one of our nastiest words, *heresy*. Try to make cultus the sum of it, and we degenerate directly into that unlovely formalism and externalism which seek to capture and domesticate the eternal so as to diminish its demands to manageable proportions; having embroidered the correct napkin in which we bury our talent, we take comfort in having done our duty. Fingers are often pointed at Anglicans for doing just this, and justice demands that we confess to having often hidden behind 'our incomparable liturgy.' But the same justice demands that the blame be shared by all other Christians, whether their liturgy is incomparable or just deplorable, who take comfort that the faithful performance of their cultic duties, whatever the manner of their execution, adequately responds to God's redemption so that life may then go on as it will until the next stated occasion.

It is possible to do the same thing with theology, and one hears the clacking of many tongues about this. It is a dreadful prospect, of course, to consider what comes out of the attempt to free theology from its cultic and ethical complications, for this way lies the most arid sophistry, ultimately even a possibly urbane but still heartless cynicism. At the very least, one's perspective becomes tragically distorted: witness the confusion in some quarters produced by the careless exchange of psychoanalytical insights, concepts, and terms with those of theology without any thinking through of their total respective meanings and implications. Be sure of it: man can no more live by brain alone than he can by bread. My only question here is simply, are we as a matter of fact guilty of the obvious kind of disembodied and irrelevant intellectualism of the stereotype? I think not: it is not true of the parish clergy whom I know in my own branch of Christianity or in others; it is not true of the intellectual centers, the seminaries and schools of divinity both denominational and otherwise which I have come to know as student, visitor, or faculty member. Is not our prevailing heresy, our popular distortion in the area of theology, the attempt to escape from theology and its demand of forthright asking and plain answering? In our acceptance of the anti-intellectualism of the age have we not actually settled upon some mysterious entity called 'the Christian Faith,' with content largely unspecified as to logical order or historical basis, but tenaciously and enthusiastically held and tensely, emotionally put forth as 'the answer'? If I do not totally mistake what many Christians are actually proclaiming today, it is this partial gospel of unreasoned, untheological commitment, substituted for theology, and itself represented as the sum and substance of Christian allegiance. Even the best and most adventurous theology cannot claim to stand alone, much less the second-rate kind.

It is equally bad when one tries to make ethics the whole concern, for once *ethos* assumes the dominance over *logos* the most sour and fault-finding moralism results. It may be good and true to remark, as we know from history, that the people of the Bible stood out in sharp distinction from their contemporaries in the ancient world for the very strictness and loftiness of their moral standards. It may even be all very well for us in this country to claim that the American people became great through the sternness of character of men with New England consciences, or, as it may be, negativistic Bible-belt morality. We must still maintain that stringent ethics serve creatively only when its cultic and theological context is preserved; and the ghastliness of the rock-ribbed conscience or the teetotal avoidance of temptations becomes apparent when the weekly churchgoing and daily Bible reading which supported them fall into disuse, as in our own time. Otherwise, we have mere accusation and even self-righteousness.

Cult, theology, ethics: these three together make up our response, at least to the extent that we can from this side of things 'make' a response. It is little enough as it is; for, of course, the complete response to the grace of God is not something of our production but of God's: the complete response is Jesus Christ incarnate, crucified, risen, and ascended. Into this response the best and most inclusive response which we can make is taken by that Saviour who in love wills to make our offering part of His. He takes our cult, theology, and ethics, along with all that we make those categories stand for, and takes them unto Himself, who is more than all our categories put together. For this reason supremely no part of the response can rightly claim the importance of the whole.

In Scripture, which provides us with the rule for our faith and conduct because it gives us the narration and interpretation of history which are definitive for us as Christians, we find all three of our categories: cult, theology, and ethics are all there. The Bible is all three in one Scripture. We have two testaments, and they in turn contain many documents, strands of tradition, and literary types of material. The varieties of its authorship, life-situations, intended readers, and special pleadings are familiar to all its serious students. It is still one Scripture, and the faith of Christians enables us to perceive this unity in Scripture's central figure, gathering all the kaleidoscopic variety of its content into one coherence. It would be untrue to the multiplicity of the Bible's content to try to find all the components of this unity in any one book, any one testament, or any single document, for the emphases come and go and are seldom all there at once in complete balance. There are, to be sure, those peaks of achievement in which the inclusiveness of the author's view and the loftiness of his insight bring us close to the point of having, for all practical purposes, all Scripture in one book: we have, for instance, the astounding masterpieces of the poem of Job and the Gospel according to Saint John. Close as they come to saying it all at once, the final, all-inclusive unity must be sought in the whole as gathered into one Christ, for most Biblical books are quite partial in their single insights. Some are largely cultic in content, like Leviticus, or in the form in which they now confront us display their former use as cultic material, like Deuteronomy and the Synoptic Gospels. Some are largely theological with long, uninterrupted passages, like Second Isaiah, the Epistle to the Romans, and the Epistle to the Hebrews. In others the ethical challenge stands out sharply: we have Amos, Jeremiah, and, if not so intense none the less urgent, the Epistle of James.

Temperament, training, and habits of thought impel all of us habitually and all but permanently to one or another of these categories as the most important, the one to which all the others can ultimately be subordinated. Sometimes change of mood or of circumstance can make this or that aspect of Biblical content more appealing and meaningful. However it may be, we must take care that, whether characteristically or temporarily one or another of the aspects of the response to grace heaves higher for us, no one part of the Bible may be read without the realization of its total context. To fail to keep this in mind is to misuse the Bible and to sidestep the full impact of the whole message as all unified in Him who is its unity.

A wholesome kind of thinking it through, however, will keep us from over-reaching ourselves in a superabundantly ambitious effort to be all things at once, to make all our teaching, preaching, and praying simultaneously and equally cultic, theological, and ethical. Even in the highest reaches of achievement in its best books, the Bible itself is not in any one book all of these at once. The emphasis of this one is completed, balanced, and highlighted by the differing emphasis of that one, and the attention is drawn for the most part to one point at one time. The lesson of this for the relationship between the differing members of the corporate body of the Church is an obvious one ever since St. Paul pointed it out, in parallel language, for the Christians in Corinth: the wholeness of the congregation is found, not in the individual excellence of the members taken singly, but in their common sharing, their pooling their resources in Christ.

And it is quite the same thing for the individual person as he seeks to find a manageable unity of all the different impulses, interests, and attractions that draw him in many directions throughout his days, and would even make many different persons of him if they could. The many things that we are and do seldom coincide, it seems. When they do meet at all, it is usually in conflict rather than in harmony. Such is the many-leveled life we have to live nowadays. When we find ourselves trying to balance out our own personality, to make all the things we are fit together, or find coherence in the person of those we know and love, we must find the ultimate unity of the person,—that coherence which makes him make sense—not in this or that single trait or aspect of him, but in that whole person whom we can truly know only as we accept him in the faith by which love perceives and understands, that whole person who each of us has become by being accepted in Christ's redeeming love.

What is this we are saying? It is that, whether we speak of the Bible, or of persons, or, as now, of the Eucharist, the value and greatness of each lies not in its possession of some single trait or group of them, but in the whole, perceived and accepted in faith and love. I must maintain this with special emphasis here because the usual course of discussions of the Eucharist is too exclusively in the area of the cultic. We habitually think of the Eucharist as something done in the sacred precincts of the Church, just as, when careless, we think of the Bible as the weapon whose ammunition of official teaching is simply to be triggered on demand. To speak of the Eucharist in its cultic significance alone is to belie the actual presence within the cultic pattern (at least in the Anglican forms familiar to us) of the theological and the ethical, and even worse to obscure the direct and immediate relevance of the cultic action of the Eucharist to the whole life and concern of the people who in the Eucharistic action bring to focus their response to redemption. The importance of the Eucharist is not to be found only in its cultic faithfulness to the relived tradition, only in its obediently offering, breaking, blessing, pouring, and receiving, even if this is the essential outline of the action. It would be ridiculous to insist that the action should at all points be simultaneously and equally cultic, theological, and ethical; but it is no worse to limit our attention to the cultic activity alone.

Just like the Bible, the Eucharist is now one, now the other. It is patent to see that the essential cultic outline proceeds directly to its business of recalling and reliving the action of the night of Christ's betrayal. But consider the language which accompanies these actions: it is language which speaks, in the formulas known to us here, of the presentation of self, soul, and body along with the rest of the oblation, and this in faith that the same Christ who presides as Lord over every Eucharist will incorporate this offering of ours into His own offering to the Father's glory, so that we may be looked on as found in Him. Immediately this has become more than cultic. The language of the prayers, interpretive and explanatory, is theological language. Even when it refuses to yield a single, consistent theological point of view, it conveys in that very ambiguity a certain theological teaching and position. It is now cultic, now theological, so that, as the Church performs the cultic actions, it speaks the words which articulate the Church's faith in what it is doing: there is more of the theological in the Eucharist, then, than just the recitation of the Creed.

Likewise, the ethical element in the Eucharist is hardly limited to the recitation of the summary of the Law at the beginning or to the exhortation of the sermon at the midpoint in the service. Only reflect on the language of the prayer for the Church which accompanies the otherwise purely cultic action of offertory. Here the Church demonstrates the sense of responsibility for society as a whole which immediately draws the lines of relevance straight from the altar, for instance, to the government, the economic life, the distressed elements of society. This means that the whole area of life beyond the ecclesiastical is involved in the Eucharistic oblation, that whole area which personal and social ethics seeks to sanctify.

The Eucharist is now the one, now the other of our categories of response. It is seldom all of them at once, the limitations of human language being what they are. But in that very shift of emphasis and inclusiveness of content we can perceive how it is that, when we say 'Eucharistic worship,' we are actually saying 'Eucharist-centered living.' Doing the action of the Eucharist in its full form means a full life in all aspects of being, all centered round the focal meeting-point at the Eucharist. It is not that God is confined or pettily localized at this point, for the very heart of the meaning of Eucharistic life is that the cultic action of the Eucharist is the point with immediate connections to all areas of life. The continuing contact of God incarnate with His world, then, is not limited to the consecrated matter of the Sacrament or even to the confines of the ecclesiastical community in its traditionally defined forms. God's continuing contact with His world is the total Eucharistic life of His people, individually and collectively considered, from their innermost raptures of devotion to their most out-going personal and social witness. This is the extension of the Incarnation of which we often hear, if one wishes to use that kind of language; or, perhaps more adequately expressed, this is the sacramental, Eucharistic application of the Incarnation to the world's continuing ages.

It is in this all-inclusive comprehensiveness toward the whole of life that we find that great single purpose which makes Eucharist and Bible share a common significance. Here we do not say, in the manner of those who would reduce it all to some simple, coon-creek formula, that it 'all comes down to' responding to redemption. This is not some simple, elementary matter to which the great complexities of Biblical record and Eucharistic worship can be reduced. In fact, it is only in the recognition of the full complexity of them both that we can find that kinship which makes Eucharist and Bible harmoniously congruent. It is only as we see in them both the same demand for total consecration of every aspect of living to the life of thanksgiving for redemption, expressed in sound thinking and right living, that we find how Eucharist and Bible do share a common unity which runs unerringly through their respective shifts and variations of emphasis.

This response to redemption is not all of its aspects at once, but they are all there in the whole. All of this response is, when its full scope is perceived, the action of the Body of

Christ, that Christ who is the full, God-given response to the Father and whose Spirit fills and guides His Body. Our living of the Eucharistic life in this awareness will enable us to perceive that the pattern of the response to grace sketched out in definitive manner in Scripture becomes an actual fact in the altar-based, witness-bearing life of Eucharist, the life of cultic, theological, ethical thanks to the God who giveth us the victory in our Lord Jesus Christ.

III

THE EUCHARIST AND EDUCATION

Dora Phyllis Chaplin, S.T.D.

Assistant Professor of Pastoral Theology,
The General Theological Seminary

THE EUCHARIST AND EDUCATION

LET us begin by asking two questions. How can we deal with so vast a subject as 'The Eucharist and Education' in a single short paper? And, what have I, an ordinary lay teacher, to offer to those who already have so much? I am impelled to attempt the impossible because of my conviction that the learner's response to God's offering of Himself in the Eucharist is the end toward which all that is taught in the life of the Church must be directed.

As to the usefulness of my laywoman's view, I remember in seriousness the responsibility of every one of us in the royal priesthood, and in gaiety the reply of Cardinal Newman to the angry bishop. Perhaps you remember what that was. The discouraged bishop said, 'The laymen, what are they?'

And the Cardinal replied, 'You must admit that without them the Church would look rather foolish!'

So it was that I came to set down a few thoughts.

As we begin, two episodes come to my mind. The first of these was a visit I made to one of our Church boarding schools for boys. On a certain evening I had addressed an assembly of the students with their parents and teachers. When the meeting was over and every other adult had disappeared, I found myself in the common room surrounded by boys. They seemed to be everywhere, on the chairs and sofas and especially on the floor. They began asking questions they had not raised at the meeting, and nearly every query was an expression of honest doubt. I said, 'But you have Sacred

43

Studies, don't you? Do you ask these questions in class or at any other time?'

The chief spokesman said, 'Some of us tried saying, when we did our written work, that we just didn't believe a whole lot of what we were taught, and we got low marks. Now we say what we are expected to say, and our grades are fine.'

Here were boys in a Church school, regular communicants, many of whose teachers were ordained men. The outward conformity of the students was hiding as much rebellion, confusion, and misunderstanding of the Faith (particularly in the area of the relationship of science to religion, and in the relevance of Christianity to life as a whole) as I have found anywhere.

The second incident was the visit of a priest to a sixty-year old woman whose husband had died suddenly at the point of retirement. She had for many, many years been a regular communicant, a generous donor of money, and indefatigable worker in the parish; she was president of this-and-that organization, and delegate to important conventions. She said to her parish priest, 'Why did this have to happen to us? I've always done so much for the Church.'

The priest made several pastoral calls and before long they were talking about the Eucharist. As he helped her to think into its meaning, she said with astonishment, 'I didn't know that this is what it is all about. Why have I lived so long and not known this?'

We might dismiss both illustrations with a quick answer, but are these the only explanations? The boys, some may say, should have been given an opportunity for discussion; this would have cured everything. For the activist lady, the same remedy might be prescribed; or it can be suggested that only crisis can teach, by making us ready to hear.

Is it not true that outward conformity and inward rebellion, or an inner vacuum, which is harder to deal with, is not an uncommon thing in all levels of parish life, in spite of much hard work on the part of the clergy and other teachers? This passive conformity, even in parishes grown proud of the centrality of the Eucharist emphasized in their liturgical customs and in the physical appointments of the church buildings, is a fact which must still be acknowledged. How may the incredulous, the indifferent, and the unaware be transformed from silent onlookers to active worshippers?

Now the Sacraments are a tremendous reality or they are nothing. It is surely the birthright of every Christian that he shall be helped to participate, as fully as he is able, in the Eucharistic worship of the Church, and to find in it the consummation of all that is good and joyful and creative in his entire existence. To do this, he must not be a spectator who stands afar off, but one who *enters into* his inheritance as a member of the Body of Christ, sharing realities which can be found only in the Holy Communion. This is a question of spiritual life—or death.

In Stephen Vincent Benét's play, *A Child Is Born*, the innkeeper's wife and some of her friends were sitting up keeping a watch on the night of the Nativity. They were restless. They were disturbed by the feeling that great unearthly events were taking place. The innkeeper's wife, who had more insight than the others, described their condition, which is ours also:

> God pity us indeed, for we are human,
> And do not always see
> The vision when it comes, the shining change,
> Or, if we see it, do not follow it,
> Because it is too hard, too strange, too new,
> Too unbelievable, too difficult,
> Warring too much with common, easy ways,

And now I know this, standing in this light,
Who have been half alive these many years,
Brooding on my own sorrow, my own pain,

.   .   .

Life is not lost by dying! Life is lost
Minute by minute, day by dragging day,
In all the thousand, small, uncaring ways,
The smooth appeasing compromises of time.[1]

It would seem to me that we too readily forget the fiery power, the love and glory with which God fulfills His promises. We are all to some extent affected by our cellophane-wrapped, synthetic civilization, because we are complacent in our substitutes for reality, and have lost our sense of adventure. In a world preoccupied with technology and industrialization, there is even a movement to manipulate human relationships by a kind of chemical reaction which attempts to make artificially constructed group life and 'fellow-shipping.' But the Church has always had to deal with the incredulous, the indifferent, and the unaware; even we who teach are at times among them. We should not idealize antiquity by entertaining romantic ideas about the conditions for handing on the Faith which existed in any period of history. This has been the Church's challenge in *all* ages.

I do not believe that there is such a thing as a 'new method' of communicating that Faith; nor do I think that any fads in teaching—and by this I mean preoccupation with one particular technique, however good in itself, to the exclusion of others—will hasten the Kingdom. For there is really only one

[1] Stephen Vincent Benét, *A Child Is Born,* from *We Stand United and Other Radio Scripts* (Rinehart). Copyright, 1942, by Stephen Vincent Benét. Quoted by permission.

method that works. As William Temple so often said, only God can do the work of God. Foolish creatures that we are, we try to do supernatural work with our natural power, blind to the truth that we shall be used to bring men to God in Christ only as our human minds and wills come under the domination of God the Holy Spirit through whom all supernatural power is given. All our plans for education will be 'without form and void' unless we recognize that central meeting place from which man derives the power of God to do the work of God. That central meeting place is in the Holy Communion.

The Church has always seen the world in realistic terms. Is not its concept of sacramental grace rooted in a recognition of our utter helplessness apart from God and His compassion for our plight? Here I am reminded of another statement by William Temple: 'Grace is not something other than God, imparted by Him; it is the very Love of God (which is Himself) approaching and seeking entry to the soul of man.'[2]

But participation in the Christian life of grace presupposes preliminary and continuing education. We know that, in the first days of the Christian Church, the catechumens heard kerygmatic preaching and received teaching from Christian leaders, with stress on fasting, penance, and discipline of life. When we look at the five areas of instruction in our Catechism—i.e. membership, faith, conduct, worship, and sacraments—we may suppose that these headings, too, might be described as the 'curriculum' of the early catechumens. From the very beginning, as Father Bouyer points out, it was 'an initiation into the life of the Church, carried out in the form of an initiation into the celebration of the liturgy.'[3] As the

[2] *Nature, Man and God* (Macmillan, 1935), p. 485.

[3] L. Bouyer, *Liturgical Piety* (University of Notre Dame Press, 1955), p. 31.

years went by, we know that many of the Fathers wrote catechetical works, and we find Saint Augustine advising those
who taught to make Christianity attractive to the learners
through the interpretation of the Bible, reminding them that
the catechumens will spend a whole lifetime with the Bible
in their liturgical worship.

Eight hundred years later, the Bishops are still concerned,
we might even say worried. In a canon written at the Council of Béziers in 1246, they say: '. . . see to it that they [i.e. the
clergy] explain to the people on Sundays the articles of faith
in simple and clear fashion so that no one may claim a veil
of ignorance. . . . Children too from seven upwards [shall be]
brought to Church by their parents on Sundays and feasts.'[4]
Twelve years later we find a request appended to the canon:
it is suggested that 'other reliable and prudent persons' help
the ordained catechists. (This call for Sunday School teachers
has been repeated every September ever since!) In the latter
part of the Middle Ages many devotional works were written
for parents reminding them that the home must be the first
school. I was delighted to find one, *Der Seelenführer* (Mainz,
1498), which, after admonishing the mothers to attend to
their duty, tells the fathers to question their children as to
how much they learned from the Sunday sermon and then
to add their 'own observations thereto.'[5] (When this is suggested in our current parish bulletins, we think that a
wonderful new idea has been born!)

Actually any systematic instruction of children seems to
have been very rare before the Council of Trent. We presume that they, like their elders (few of whom could read

[4] G. S. Sloyan (ed.), *Shaping the Christian Message, Essays in
Religious Education* (Macmillan, 1959), p. 27.

[5] Ibid. p. 42, cited by J. A. Jungmann.

or write) learned most of what they knew of Christianity from what they heard or misheard and from what they saw in stained glass and pictures in their churches. Hence, perhaps, the growth of much superstition. Like our young people, they were visual-minded. They saw sacred plays, and mumming, processions on the frequent feast days, and litany processions in times of disaster. The Eucharist was constantly brought into their thoughts—for instance, in the processions of guild members, the bakers went first because their work entailed the handling of the bread. Meals and mourning, festivity and famine, all were closely related to the parish church, and the pageantry of the Christian year.

The fainter echoes were still there in my own English childhood when the church bell would toll at a neighbor's death: there were double strokes for a woman and triple for a man, and it was perfectly natural to hear a grown-up say, 'Ah, that must be Mr. So-and-so, I know he has been very ill.' We would go on with our play, unconsciously accepting death as a part of life. The goose that was roasted at Michaelmas, the puddings made on Stir-up Sunday, the Sunday next before Advent, the violets we gathered on Mothering Sunday and the primroses at Easter, were accepted as very ordinary customs. In the church, there were the great sheaves of wheat and baskets of fruit at the Harvest Thanksgiving. Here all of life was our religious teacher—because all of life was related to the Church.

In the education of God's people, you can see some threads that run through the centuries; certain basic things needed to be understood: for the Jews, God's laws and covenant; for the Christians, the great news of the atoning life of Christ, the New Covenant, and the New Life shared in Christ after baptism into His death and resurrection. As time went on, there was catechetical material to be learned. But the Church could never be satisfied with the mere articulation of *dogma*. It has always known that these basic religious facts must be related to the whole of human life. As it was during the time of the writing of the Book of Deuteronomy, parents have been exhorted to teach in the home; and the *doctrine*, the knowledge which becomes a part of our deepest unconscious life, those things which we take for granted in families and communities, have a formative influence we cannot measure. We, as they, are teaching too. However poorly or however well, we cannot avoid teaching by work and example. In our advertising, entertainment, journalism, and conversation, especially in our table talk at home, whether these things be stumbling blocks or stepping stones, we are always teaching.

If we are to learn anything we must become involved in it. Take any topic—arithmetic, for instance. You will need a teacher, a course, and a technique. But if it is to open up the pupil's mind and truly educate (using the word as it was originally conceived, from *educere*, a leading out or bringing out), the learner enters into the subject so that it may become a reality to him. The student and his subject have become one. With most subjects the learner will have become involved in it, but not as a whole person. Arithmetic cannot answer the ultimate questions of life and death.

But envision the fact of Christ as the object of our student's education. Again, the learner enters into the subject. His technique is his worship, his participation in the Eucharistic liturgy. He loses himself and enters into the actual substance of his topic. The learner and his subject are one. The fact of Christ is the subject known and entered into. The learner knows Christ's life and he shares it; his whole person is caught up in Christ. For he is, as it were, involved in Him, in God Himself. Now he finds the ultimate truth and in doing so he finds himself, for at last he knows himself to be a son of God. He finds that Christ shows the way to God for He Himself is the Way. Alice Meynell describes the journey in her *I Am the Way*:

> Thou art the Way
> Hadst Thou been nothing but the goal,
>   I cannot say
> If Thou hadst ever met my soul.

. . .

> I'll not reproach
> The road that winds, my feet that err
>   Access, Approach
> Art Thou, Time, Way, Wayfarer.[6]

And Christopher Fry puts it thus:

> The enterprise
> Is exploration into God.[7]

This is Christian education. And Christ becomes known to us in the Breaking of the Bread.

The pattern for our educational procedure is found within the liturgy. God the Holy Spirit teaches through His Church: priest and people, the whole family of God worshipping in an atmosphere of profound devotion and *koinonia*. The course is the liturgy itself. There is first the proclamation of the atoning Life made in Epistle, Gospel, Creed, and sermon; then comes what we saw as the end of all education, the entering into the New Life, when Christ repeats the Ascension

[6] *The Poems of Alice Meynell,* Complete Edition (Oxford University Press, 1940), p. 80.

[7] *A Sleep of Prisoners* (Oxford University Press, 1951), p. 49.

in us and we have a foretaste of life lived in the Kingdom. God *reveals* to us what He intended us to be and sends us back into the world to *be* what He intended us to be. Through His grace we have received reality.

The liturgy is not only the educational process *par excellence*, it is the center and substance of all Christian teaching. We must be clear about this, for sometimes we hear the Parish Communion, for instance, referred to as though it were an educational resource or a device. This is blasphemy. In the Incarnation, we have the perfect union of creation and Creator. In the liturgy, creation is once more lifted up to the Creator. God continues to give Himself to us, as He did supremely in the Incarnation. In the Eucharist His self-giving is continuously expressed and enters the lives of men. We are concerned not with a scheme but with a Person.

I am convinced that all teachers, ordained and unordained, must prepare their pupils to *respond* to God's grace. Christ's work *for* us must become Christ's work *in* us. The people in the illustrations I gave at the beginning—the schoolboys and the older woman—were unable to participate in the full sacramental life because they were unable to respond. J. S. Whale, in his *Christian Doctrine*, makes a strong statement which teachers may well ponder. He says:

The grace of the Gospel is not a 'thing,' a sort of spiritual 'bloodplasm' for distribution to men through the channels of the sacramental system: a divine 'stuff,' so to speak, . . . working in magically objective fashion on the soul of the Communicant, without conscious response on his part, just as aspirin might work on his body. . . . The grace of God is mediated not so much through faith as to faith.[8]

---

[8] (Macmillan, 1941), pp. 162–3.

Later he says, 'God acts redemptively through his Church and his Sacraments; man responds by faith.'[9] In the words of the liturgy, 'Feed on him in thy heart by faith, with thanksgiving.'

We now turn to the practical application of all this. How may those we teach be helped through faith and thanksgiving to overcome the obstacles which hinder them from entering into the New Life in Christ? Here are a few suggestions drawn from my experience.

1. *A reverence for all life must be encouraged in the Christian student.* This is closely related to our response to God in worship. Some learn to reverence other living things (including animals and plants and the whole created world, as well as people) from their early childhood, because they acquire the Christian attitudes of adults around them. Others receive an un-Christian education. They learn on the unconscious levels that the rest of creation exists to be exploited for their own ends. If they change at a later time of spiritual rebirth, it is because they discover that they and all other men are created by God and valued by God. The people with whom we live and eat and work, those we employ or by whom we are employed, fellow committee members, and those we teach, are immortals making the same journey as ourselves. Father Guardini, in *The Church and the Catholic*, exclaims: 'How deep must be the knowledge one can have of another! ... because the lives of both are rooted in the same ultimate realities. One can help another, because he no longer need find reasons for trusting him.'[10]

[9] Ibid. p. 164.

[10] R. Guardini, *The Church and the Catholic and the Spirit of the Liturgy* (translated by Ada Lane; Sheed and Ward, 1935), p. 97.

Out of reverence for life comes awe, wonder, and thanks-giving which we can offer in the liturgy in the language of praise. It leads to the adoration of God, and love for God. Children should not spend countless hours of their lives being entertained, while they are shut away from created things, from the natural world. They should be given time for crea-tive work and play and thinking. Imagination is closely allied to our ability to reach out to the unseen, the first step across the barrier of the useful and the obvious, to find the glory of God shining behind all life.

In the sacramental universe where we live, we find that the spiritual and material do not run on parallel lines; they inter-act in every moment of our lives. Consider what this means to the worshipper who makes his communion every Sunday. If he has not learned to live thankfully wherever he may be, he cannot suddenly begin to offer on Sunday what he has carefully withheld every other day of the week. But if he has come to know that existence itself is sacred, that he is related to God on all levels of physical and mental life, then the many parts of his days—whether they be words, things, acts, thoughts— have been recognized as sacramentals in prepara-tion for the Sacrament. Is it not true that learners are often asked to express at the altar praise and thanksgiving which they do not bring with them?

You remember the story in Genesis 28, when Jacob on his journey lies down to sleep, a heap of stones for his pillow. In verse 16 we read:

And Jacob awaked out of his sleep, and he said, Surely the Lord is in this place; and I knew it not. And he was afraid, and said, How dreadful is this place! this is none other but the house of God, and this is the gate of heaven.

Here we have holy fear. We may think of it as an allegorical description of the time when we come to see that 'heaven lies all about us.' God Himself leads us across the frontier which lies between us and a larger universe.

I have always cherished a story told by Evelyn Underhill of a Scottish gardener who asked a lady just returned from a journey where she had been. When she replied that she had visited the island of Iona, he said, 'Ah, Iona is a very thin place.' When the lady inquired what he meant, he said, 'It's thin because there's very little between Iona and the Lord.'

Through the adoration of God, we come to see that every place is a 'thin' place. Through the new eyes of worship we know that the whole of God's universe is penetrated by Him, and the glory which was always there becomes apparent. One small flower expressed this mystery for a poet who said:

> Slight as thou art, thou art enough to hide
> > Like all created things, secrets from me,
> > And stand a barrier to eternity.
>
> .   .   .
>
> Thou little veil for so great mystery,
> > When shall I penetrate all things and thee
> And then look back? . . .
> > > > what will it be to look
> > From God's side even of such a simple thing? [11]

Only those who have within themselves a growing reverence for all life should teach.

2. *There must be a foundation of right belief.* We have considered how the spirit of worship and adoration may grow, but I would like to stress the necessity for sound theological roots for teaching and preaching. I am thinking of theology here as the fact of God and His revelation to men. E. R. Mascall, in *He Who Is, A Study in Traditional*

[11] *The Poems of Alice Meynell*, p. 56 ('To a Daisy').

Theism, maintains that it is too often assumed that people 'inherit, as by a kind of birthright, at least the essential elements of the Christian doctrine of God.' He says later that

... the doctrine of God is the basis upon which all other Christian doctrine rests, any error that has been allowed to creep into a man's belief about God will distort his understanding of every other Christian truth. If his idea of God is wrong, his idea of Christ will be wrong, since Christ is God incarnate; and his ideas of the Church and Sacraments will be wrong, since the Church is Christ's Body and the Sacraments are the instruments of his action upon the human soul.[12]

Many fall away from the Church, or continue to go through the outward motions of worshipping, unable to respond to God because they hide within themselves dislike, distrust, petrifying fear, and even hatred of the One about whom they are misinformed. We often bring our childish notions into adult life. These ideas may have come through poor teaching, unhappy experiences, or bad art, or just ignorance of what the Faith is. They may come through those who have given the impression that religion is a dull pretense or a sentimental fantasy. (Imagine, for instance, what happens when church-goers proclaim to the young and to the stranger looking in, 'Here is fullness of life.' The newcomers may well look in upon some of the Church's activities and say, 'Is this the fullness of life of which you speak?')

Care should be taken all along the way that a sound doctrine of God is taught. The task of formal teaching should not be handed over indiscriminately to the well meaning. It is the warped and infantile ideas coming from the older generation that find their way into many of the so-called Christian courses of study for the young.

[12] (Longmans, Green, 1954), pp. 2–3.

Right belief should not be taken for granted. I would respectfully suggest that since the priest is, or should be, the last instructor of parishioners before their Confirmation, he should remind himself several times a day that *his people have not had several years of formal theological education.* He must constantly think his theology through *from the beginning,* or he will lose touch with the learners. Naturally, the extent of formal teaching given will be determined by the ages and academic ability and needs of the confirmands. Whatever the academic education of the students may have been, there is always a need for a teacher who can go back and stand among the catechumens.

All teachers need to develop the ability to go up and down the spiral staircase of what they know. Imagine such a staircase in a tower. With each turn of the stair, as you climb it, you may look out of the window and see a wider and clearer view of God's world and His fulfilled promises. We might even say you can enjoy God more and more.

When you were a child, you were at the bottom. If in your teens you learned to harmonize your growing ideas of history and science you moved higher. As your knowledge of theology grew, you moved at a great rate, and when you passed your canonicals still wider vistas opened up before you.

Teachers must not forget how they arrived at a particular place on the staircase. They must be able to run down and meet the other climbers and move up with them. In other words, they must remember the beliefs they once held and how they grew more mature.

Current jargon has already had its effect on the confirmand before he comes to you. The kind of prayers he will pray depends upon the kind of God he believes in. When we come to the altar, we need to be able to *open* our lives to receive Him, to come with love and hope to a God we trust.

3. *Communicants need to learn more about the shape of the Eucharistic liturgy.* Many instructions that are given remind one of a guide in a cathedral who takes the tourist behind a choir stall to examine a tiny vein on a hidden leaf carved there long ago. He spends so much time on this detail that they never come to see the great sweeps of the arches. This shows in 'instructed Eucharists' where an attempt is made to give so much excellent and detailed information that the congregation is unable to remember any of it. It is far better to take one theme at a time—for example, Offering—and to impress it upon the hearts and minds of the hearers as one great movement of the Eucharistic drama. Later, when the essential pattern is seen in outline, the details can come.

Those who have long known the words of the liturgy by heart and are familiar with its structure forget the time when the prayers seemed long and unrelated and the unfolding of the drama was obscure. The relation of the parts is clearly shown in the Associated Parishes publication, *The Parish Eucharist*. It needs to be recalled often to the minds of the worshippers, never taken for granted.

Miles L. Yates, in his invaluable little manual *Our Bounden Duty*, divides the two main sections in a way that is helpful. Part 1 is described simply as

We THINK of what God wants of us as Christ revealed it,

and Part 2 is divided into stages:

We GIVE OURSELVES to God [Offertory]

OUR SELF-GIVING IS ACCEPTED in union with Christ's Perfect Offering [Consecration]

God GIVES HIMSELF to us [Communion]

ending with thanksgiving:

We THANK God for what He did and does for us in Christ,

adding that 'Christ sends us out from *Communion* to help create *community*.'[13]

This knowledge is only a way to a fuller participation in God's gifts, just as our appreciation of a symphony is enhanced when we understand a little of its structure. At the time of the communion, whether for the scholar or the unlearned, there must be a simplicity about our reception of God's gift, a naturalness. When we meet a much-loved person, it is not good to be thinking, 'I wonder if I am doing the right thing, if my friend is pleased with me, if our friendship is real and will last, if I am worthy of such a privilege.' If these are our preoccupations, we shall not be able to respond to the love that is offered.

There are unfathomable riches for those who want to explore the endless paths opened up in the liturgy; yet there will always be many, perhaps a majority, who find what they know best expressed in the famous quatrain:

> Christ was the Word that spake it,
> He took the bread and brake it;
> And what that Word did make it,
> I do believe and take it.

4. *We must be realistic and face the problem of meaninglessness in modern lives.* Life today is often far removed from created things. It has for many become artificial, remote from the natural rhythm of the seasons. The splendid panorama of spring and fall, for instance, is barely perceptible in the cities where most people live. Our food, our entertainment, our

[13] *Our Bounden Duty, A Manual of Devotion for Communicants* (Oxford University Press, 1951), pp. 9–14.

very thoughts are in danger of becoming artificial, like dice loaded to fall a certain way, weighted by advertising and the popular press. I do not mean that a return to the country would automatically cure us of ills. We would not necessarily be able to see the beauty around us; our vision might well be blurred. (Witness those who flee to their country cabins and immediately equip them with television.) Many of us have been torn away from our contact with nature and have been robbed of those things which give us reasons for wonder. Christianity provides others.

Knowledge of science can rekindle our wonder. It can bring us to adore God and to desire a way of life that will help us to fulfill the ultimate purposes of the Creator; it leads us to see that the physical universe is a manifestation of ultimate reality. It is as though God beckons to us through all truth and all beauty.

Through the Christian year the liturgy restores to us the rhythm of the seasons, day by day. No matter whether formal classes are the custom in a parish, or whether everyone receives instruction on other occasions, all teaching needs to be set against its background. Let young and old enter once again into its color and music and customs, and let them be carried into the home. They may be ancient customs, but in this generation new ways can be found in which to interpret them. The Roman Catholic Church has done much more than we have in this direction. I wish we might produce an Anglican magazine for Christian parents and teachers as excellent as *The Altar and the Home,* published by the Roman Benedictines. We must keep life in the home closely related to the Eucharist. For as Gerald Vann reminds us often: 'It is Christianity which uses and blesses the stone, the wood, the bread, the wine, the water, the oil, and in doing so teaches us incidentally to treasure and to understand the great basic human realities of love and sex, of home and hearth, of friendship and hospitality, the soil and seasons and sun and stars.'[14] Miles L. Yates in *The King in His Beauty* describes the Christian year happily. He says:

I am not sure that there is anything like it in the world: this composite of sanctities, this interweaving of story and prayer, of song and color, by which Christ is portrayed and brought before us. It is a solemn pageantry which effects association with Him whose life is being traced. It is a solemn processional in which we actually move in spirit. It is an annual miracle . . .[15]

So the Christian once more discovers his roots in the universe, and recovers his faculty of wonder and joy.

5. *The sacramental principle must be better understood by both teachers and learners.* It is not a question as to whether we believe in the sacramental idea or not. It is built into the whole of life and we cannot escape it. We need to identify it, to know that it runs through all of life and that there is nothing strange or esoteric about it. It runs through all our ties with one another, at home, in our social life, in commerce, and in international relationships. We see outward forms with inward meanings, from common little sacramental signs like handshakes to elaborate pageantry.

The student may be helped to see that while we live in a time-space world we know reality chiefly through our senses. We certainly do most of our communicating with each other through material means—the tongue speaks, the ears hear, we talk, we write, we project our ideas on a screen, we telephone—all these means of communicating with one an-

---

[14] *The Water and the Fire* (Collins, 1953), p. 155.

[15] (Seabury Press, 1957), p. 13.

other need a body to express them. The Christian must know himself to be not a spirit only, nor a body only. He is a spiritual being in his totality. He is created to live in two worlds, the world of the senses and the world of the spirit. The late Father Andrew taught his confirmands to answer the person who said, 'Do you have a soul?' by saying, 'No!' When the questioner expressed his surprise, they were to explain, 'I *am* a soul, and I *have* a body.'

God chooses outward forms to convey inner meanings, even the gift of Himself. Von Hügel expresses his awe at this miracle by saying that in the Eucharist we see 'God giving Himself through such apparently slight vehicles, in such short moments, and under such bewilderingly humble veils.'[16] Spiritual reality is brought to us through material means because that is the way we are created to receive it.

Now it takes time to learn this through worship and instruction. Both young and old must be helped to apprehend it in their own way. In our confirmation classes we too often hear a quick reference to the sacramental principle, and it is assumed that somehow the students now understand, whereas most of us need a good deal of help in this area. I have been present at confirmation classes when the instructor has said, 'We live in a sacramental universe. Be sure to write that down in your notebooks.' Shortly thereafter the class is asked to write down the names of the 'Seven Sacraments.'

The underlying principle in the life of worship cannot be brushed aside without tragic consequences. If we take time to question confirmands, we often find that they have come to divide the universe into two spheres, the spiritual and the material, and of the two the material sphere to them is *real*.

[16] F. von Hügel, *The Mystical Element of Religion, as studied in St. Catherine of Genoa and her Friends* (J. M. Dent, 1908), I, 241.

They have no awareness of the world where the spiritual and the material are mysteriously united, where, penetrated by God, the invisible is clothed with the outward and the visible; yet this is the world in which we live.

Christianity is not a 'spiritual religion,' and those who regard it as such tend to think of the whole physical world as evil. This physical world will include their own bodies and those of others. And think of the effect of this heresy on our attitude to Eucharistic worship. Dr. Casserley points out that those who accept it, see the Eucharist as a séance with our Lord present as a disembodied ghost giving us Bread and Wine. This is an example of wrong belief as a hindrance to true worship. One cannot separate faith and knowledge, for with wrong knowledge—misinformation—we are prevented from moving forward in faith. We cannot overestimate the need for good teaching.

We need people who can illumine and interpret the basic teachings of the Catechism and help learners to see them as related to all of life. Reginald Lumb did this slowly and imaginatively in his First, Second, and Third Year of the Catechism. These books were written for English children, and already some of the examples he chooses to illustrate his points are out of date. We need to have similar books written for Americans. Not everyone has the lively gifts that are required for such work; almost none can do it well without careful preparation. Those priests who see its vital importance and who have cultivated the gift of bringing dogma to life for their people will not need to say what I heard the Bishop of one big diocese say recently: 'If only we could keep *half* of our confirmands in the Church, what strength we would have!'

Actually, all that goes on in a Christian's education from birth up might be described as pre-confirmation instruction, and post-confirmation instruction. Teaching after one has begun to receive the Holy Communion is, like post-marital counseling, an opportunity for raising questions about a life into which *one has already entered,* and about which it is now possible to think in a nonacademic way. New questions come to the mind of the learner. We need good post-confirmation instruction and discussion.

Finally, we come to see once more that the foundation of all that we do lies in the celebration of the Eucharist itself. Those who teach and those who learn must participate in it. At the altar we discover not only how to teach, but there we receive the grace of God to do the work of God. And to learners of all ages, those who teach represent Christ and His Church; they stand for Him in word and deed.

Those of us who have been given the terrible responsibility and privilege of taking a small part in the education of souls pray always 'that we may evermore dwell in Him and He in us.'

IV

ECONOMIC AND SOCIAL IMPLICATIONS OF THE EUCHARIST

The Reverend Wilford Oakland Cross, Ph.D., D.D.

*Professor of Philosophy of Religion and Ethics,
The University of the South*

ECONOMIC AND SOCIAL IMPLICATIONS OF THE EUCHARIST

ETHICAL PRINCIPLES INHERENT IN THE EUCHARIST

THIS is a discussion of the social implications of the Holy Eucharist. One of the dangers of examining a topic of this nature, which deals with implications and ethical principles, is that one will fall into the fallacy of moralizing the Eucharist, making it a source for didactic principles of morality. This would entail a reduction of the value and significance of the Eucharistic rite. It would make of the Eucharist a text from which moral conclusions could be drawn. The Eucharist is not a teaching device, *per se*. Edification is the least of its values. Any teaching of a moral nature that can be drawn from it must rest upon the fact that having participated in this action certain consequences follow for the life of the participating worshipper.

The Eucharist is an intensification of the Christian life. In other words, the Christian life is Eucharistic from dawn to sunset, from sunset to dawn. It is an offering of creatureliness to Almighty God, and this daily, hourly, perpetual offering of life is intensified, epitomized, caught into dramatic action, in the Eucharistic rite. The Eucharist does not have embedded in it ethical and moral implications to be drawn, *by force,* out of it to be carried over and applied and imposed upon another realm of activity. Its social implications are not concepts and notions that have to be carried out from beneath the dim mystery of gothic arches into the sunshine of the world. Rather, life is, for the Christian, Eucharistic, sacramental, and incarnational at its very center. This relationship of Christianity to life, of grace to nature, becomes most vocal and explicit in the Eucharist, but it is in theory everywhere and every day present and regnant in the daily life of every Christian. The Eucharist is the Christian life intensified, not some ethereal mystery hovering remotely over the daily concerns of a Christian. The Eucharist, therefore, is Christian living in a liturgical mode, not a sort of whipped cream, topping life as it is lived on a mundane level.

I hope this point is not too subtle, for it is an important point. What I am trying to say is that merely sitting down and looking at the Prayer Book text of the Eucharist and pulling out passages that have moral and social reference is only the beginning of an understanding of the meaning of the Eucharist for our current social order. It is not merely a matter of saying, 'This is said on Sunday to be followed on Monday and Tuesday.' Asking the question, 'What does the Eucharist mean in the factory, the office, the home, on the golf links?' does not quite cut deep enough if the answer is merely textual. The ethical implications of the Eucharist are not merely pulled out, as if with a dentist's forceps, from the text of the Mass. They are not drawn out of the Eucharist to be artificially applied.

The ethical principles immanent within the Eucharist are the ethical principles of daily Christian living. They are involved in and are basic to the covenant into which we have entered with Almighty God. They are the terms of indenture of that covenant. The ethical principles immanent in the Eucharistic action are the Will of God for man. They are not anything special which good Catholics follow, or only sacramental devotees follow, but are principles laid down in the birth pangs of creation itself. They are implicit in the structure of the cosmos and in the nature of man. In short, the ethical and social principles of the Eucharist are the whole texture of the Divine and Natural Law. They are not a special revelation but the total ethical relevance of the Will of God for man's conduct.

It is for this reason that very early in the rite of the Eucharist the priest rehearses to the people the Commandments or the Summary of the Law, thereby enunciating, in minuscule, the whole burden of Christian ethic. This comes not as an imposition of moral imperatives but as a reminder of a covenant, freely and joyously entered into on the part of the people. In the exhortation before the confession, the priest again invokes the covenantal terms. Those who receive the sacrament are those expected to 'intend to lead a new life, following the commandments of God, and walking from henceforth in His holy ways.' At the end of the rite, also at the close of the prayer of thanksgiving for the divine gift, we pray that we may 'do all such good works as thou hast prepared for us to walk in.' None of these Prayer Book references to the moral life refer to anything other than the simplest Christian duty and service.

In essence, then, the Eucharist is not an ethical document but a marvelous poem of praise and thanksgiving. Nevertheless the very uttering of that praise and thanksgiving implies such a relationship of men to God that fulfilling His will in our lives becomes a bounden duty and service. Therefore, ethical, social, and moral action is implicit in every line of the Eucharistic ritual.

Instinctively we tend to evade the use of the Ten Commandments in the liturgy. This is to avoid, I think, the didactic, moralizing tone in worship; and I think this instinct is well founded. The Mass is not a moral lecture but the beauty of holiness. It appeals to deeper levels of our nature even than the conscience. This does not mean, on the other hand, that the Ten Commandments are inseparable from the beauty of holiness. We are told that when they were first given, the mountain smoked, thunder was heard, and the hearts of men quaked within them before the majesty of God most high. It does mean, however, that from a psychological point of view we are concerned to avoid making the Holy Communion a moral preachment or a lesson or a lecture.

Morality is not in itself dull. It answers the most practical and urgent of questions that man asks, the questions, 'How shall I live? How shall I spend the days of my life?' Nagging and fussing at people about morality is another story, however. All of us, I suppose, have inbuilt psychological mechanisms of resistance against such nagging and fussing. We survived childhood and became adult either by working out antidotes or fostering rebellion against the 'no, no' of our mothers, and some residue of that process of growing up remains with us so that we resist the 'no' of moral law as by a kind of instinct. We want to be guided, not repressed and inhibited. The Eucharist, therefore, must not be presented as a moral treatise if its positive ethical implications are to be heard and followed.

Whatever the Eucharist has to teach, then, about ethical and social matters is not something special, something, for instance, which Quakers, who have no liturgy, are not bound by, or non-liturgical Protestants are not expected to live up to. It is not something specially binding upon the historic, liturgical churches. It is as relevant for graduates from Virginia as for men from Nashotah.

What the Eucharist implies about social and economic affairs is what God demands, what Christ taught, what the Church proclaims, what the Bible teaches, what the Natural Law points to. The Eucharist sets forth the Will of God. I have labored this point because there is some danger of a debilitating tendency toward preciousness in the Liturgical Movement. By preciousness I mean an isolated, sanctuary-imprisoned type of Christianity which can only be talked about among those who know the thought-patterns and vocabulary of the Liturgical Movement. Just as disciples of Wagner can share their Wagnerianism only with Wagnerian-ites, so liturgiologists stand in some danger of communicating only with the initiated. This is probably of necessity true of ceremonial matters. But there is and cannot be a special ethic of the liturgical advance-guard. The ethic of that ad-vance-guard must be the universal ethic of all men, since ethic itself is defined among Christians, as the will of the Creator for His human creatures.

II

THE CHRISTIAN VIEW OF SOCIETY

It is true, nevertheless, that the advance-guard of the Liturgical Movement is more keenly aware of the social evangel of Christianity than a great many Christians. Romano Guardini says, in *The Church and the Catholic,* the Liturgi-cal Movement 'is a particular powerful current. . . . Through it the Church enters the life of prayer as a religious reality, and the life of the individual becomes an integral part of the life of the Church. . . . Here the individual is as one of the people.'[1]

It is this awareness of the social nature of Christianity that sent the factory priests of France into the industrial order of modern society to bring the Eucharist into close juxtaposition with the humming wheels of manufacture. This awareness of social realities has begun a revolution in church architecture in an effort to enshrine the Eucharistic action in buildings as closely in harmony with the functional characteristics of modern homes, offices, and factories as possible. Whatever we may think of the merits of the folk-music and jazz-music renditions of the sung parts of the Mass, as they have currently appeared, the advent of these attempts is a symptom of social awareness on the level of a desire to communicate, to worship in a medium 'understanded of the people.'

These efforts are the antidote for that ritual preciousness of which I spoke formerly. The relationship of the Eucharist to the life of man about us has been sharply intensified by the Liturgical Movement. The title of one great pioneer work in English in liturgical studies is very significantly *Liturgy and Society*.[2]

III

SOCIETY AND PERSONS

The Liturgical Movement has made men aware that the religion of Christ is not an individualistic, hole-in-the-corner piety. It is a communal, social enterprise within which men

[1] (Sheed and Ward, 1935), p. 28.

[2] A. G. Hebert (Faber and Faber, 1935).

are of one blood in the Mystical Body of Christ. The Eucharist is the supreme expression of this communal, brotherly tie within the Body, since Eucharistic action is the Body of Christ met to invoke and to be His power and presence.

The social nature of the Church, and hence of the Eucharist, (mirroring as Church and Eucharist do the social nature of humanity itself as sheafed together in the Creator) is not so much an ethical implication drawn from the Eucharist as it is an undergirding fact of the Eucharist. Men are of one blood. The bread is of one loaf. The Mystical Body of Christ is the union of men in the creative Logos that made them. This fact of social community is the first principle of the Eucharist.

The social implications for industrial society of this fact are not merely obvious; they are catastrophic for a social order based upon self-seeking, enlightened self-interest, isolated individualism, and the raw brutalities that under some conditions seep from the profit motive. This judgment holds for both management and labor. The first economic ethical principle which is immanent in the meaning of the Eucharist is that men are born into a social order, not a social jungle. There can be little harmony between belief in the significance of the Eucharist and the habitual Social Darwinism of the school of 'Let the strong prevail and the weak go to the wall' in an exploiting struggle of ruthless competition. Goods are not made for struggle but for the use of men. In the nineteenth century enlightened self-interest, *laissez faire* economics, and the notion of survival of the fittest drawn from biological theory were united together to create a mental image of the industrial entrepreneur as a ruthless, conquering individual.

This was the age of the Morgans, the Carnegies, and the Vanderbilts, men who almost single-handedly built vast industrial empires. The biological facts, however, that were drawn upon to support this vision of industrial triumph, had very little connection with the evolution of mankind, but much connection with the life history of *carnivora* like the tiger and the lion. However, man in trying to roar like a lion often brayed like a jackass. Man is not an individual in this carnivorous solitary sense. He has no genuine claws or fangs. His biological survival owes more to the muscles of his throat than to his equipment for battle and the chase in terms of swiftness and destructive natural weapons; survival depends on his ability to talk, to communicate with his fellows, to organize their several individual weaknesses into a team of hunters and fighters. In short, man survives by his reason and his capacity for organization. The myth of the preying beast, enunciated by the Social Darwinians, has given way in our day to philosophies of Togetherness and Belongingness to the opposite extreme of the Darwinian conqueror, to the anonymity of the Organization Man. In its turn, the factor of social co-operation has now been woefully exaggerated to the point where the very concept of individual human personality is in peril.

That man is a social animal is a salient and significant fact. It is also a salient and significant fact that he is a person.

The emphasis upon man's social nature proclaimed by the Eucharist is not an endorsement of totalitarian theory or of Togetherness. It does not countenance any philosophy of the individual being sunk in the social order, any more than it implies the mythological individualism of the nineteenth-century Social Darwinians.

Society, while it is the womb of humanity, does not in Christian teaching exist for itself but only to give birth to human persons. The Social Order is an instrument to produce the richness of human personality. The Eucharist emphasizes society, the gathering and assemblage of the Brotherhood of the Mystical Body, and thus sets forth by implication the true pattern of man's relationship to man, but the Eucharist never loses sight of the person. This personal note is struck frequently. Though the creed is a statement of corporate faith, it begins with the phrase 'I believe,' thus underlining individual commitment. This note of personal responsibility is sounded again in the Exhortation and in the Confession where individual faith, charity, and purpose of amendment are emphasized. At the reception of communion the words recited are 'given for thee.' The Eucharist is social in its very nature, being the Body of Christ offering itself but, on the other hand, sheer, unqualified 'belongingness' and 'togetherness' are never endorsed.

The Body of Christ is a molecule, but no molecule could exist except for the substantial integrity of its atoms. The primary Eucharistic implication for the relationship of man to man, therefore, is that the social order consists of a human brotherhood in which the individual person is cherished and preserved.

The Christian social philosophy, the Christian doctrine of Man, or Christian Anthropology, is thus enshrined in the Eucharistic action and in the very definition of what the Eucharist is. The Eucharist is the Body of Christ offering thanksgiving for creation and redemption to the Father. The implied social doctrine is that man is sheaved into a brotherhood in which all race, class, and status are annihilated but in which the sacredness of the human person is affirmed. This is the germ of what the social order under God should be. This view of society denies at once the truth and relevance of the violence and totalitarian statism of Marxist socialism, and at the same time equally condemns the raw, unsocial individualism of survival-of-the-fittest capitalism. Both reduce man to the status of a cog or 'hand.' This puts me in mind of an Elizabethan story. One of the Queen's sea captains reported to her after an engagement that none of his personnel had been lost, but that one hand had been shot through the nose! This flexible social principle of the molecular unity and atomic substantiality of men in society embraces obviously two poles of man's nature in a creative synthesis—the pole of his social nature and the pole of his personal autonomy. This is a delicate balance of extremes, but it is a creative balance. The truth that man owes to society his very manhood but that society exists not for itself but to produce and nourish that manhood is obviously founded both upon the Natural Law and upon Biblical revelation.

The Christian ethic, as it faces every problem in current social turmoil, discovers the key to true answers and solutions when it remembers that man is at the same time a social animal, in the fullest Aristotelian and Thomistic sense of that term, and that he is also a person with an ultimate end and goal in the life of God. The action of the Eucharist is shot through and through with this vision of the compound and composite nature of man, that he is a social being and at the same time a person. All Christian economic teaching must stem from this assertion.

IV

MAN, NATURE, AND THE INDUSTRIAL ORDER

The social implications of the Eucharist go beyond this general view of the relation of man to society. In the Eucharist the relationship of man to the earth, to cosmic nature, is also manifest. Dean Ladd of Berkeley, whose contribution to the Liturgical Movement ought not to be slighted, used to speak of the Offertory as the 'Liturgy of Creation.'

Our Prayer Book rendition of the ancient ceremonial of the Offertory is far more representative of Puritan fear of Nature than of Catholic joy in God's creation. It represents the repercussion of Luther's opinion that the Offertory stank of oblation.

However, within the rubrical chains fastened upon us we can still lift up our hands in thanksgiving for Creation. The priest is ordered to offer and to place upon the table the bread and the wine. This in itself is a recognition that the ancient Jewish rite, and indeed the rite of every nature religion, is still vital, reminding us of man's duty to render thanks for his existence. We offer upon God's altar the stuff of wheat and grape, the stuff of dust upon which our earthly life depends. Here in this gesture we make formal recognition of our creaturehood, our dependence, our tie with the earth, our structure of dust, and our nature of clay. These are God's gifts which we thankfully acknowledge. This wheat out of the earth, this juice of grape, epitomizes our gratitude for life and being, our thanksgiving for mothering earth and animating breath, our return to God of symbols of the dust out of which we are dug. In the Offertory gesture we come as creatures before our Creator upon whose existential energy our being depends.

It is essential to remember, however, that while all this is true, we do not, as a matter of fact, bring to God's altar wheat and grapes. Wheat and grapes have been transformed. Bread and wine are made of the stuff of nature, but they are no longer wheat and grapes. Human manufacture and human ingenuity have transformed them. They have been changed by human technology. Into bread has gone the arts of agriculture, of industry and commerce. It has been sown, harvested, thrashed, milled, ground, baked, transported, and sold. Our economy of agriculture, industry, finance has become involved in this substance. It is symbolic and redolent of our society. The same may be said of wine, which is not the grape but what man has made from grapes. We offer, therefore, upon the altar at once what God has given and what man has made out of His gifts. We offer, in consequence, our lives as members of a society which by enterprise and co-operative labor makes usufructs from the raw material of nature. What we offer is nature transformed by industry, dust transubstantiated by the labor of a social order.

The economic order is laid upon the altar under and through these tokens. Our culture and civilization have entered into the making of these symbols and are implicit in them. Our world lies upon the altar epitomized in this wafer of daily bread. Our very existence is caught up into this token, the primordial dust fashioned by man into the staff of life.

V

THE SIGNIFICANCE OF BREAD

Let us examine the meaning of a wafer, a host. Within this sliver of bread, at its deepest level, lies the creative energy by whose causal fiat all things are made. Beneath its surface structure, even below its atomic constituency, lies a world of sheer energy, the power in things to be. As a token of existential reality it is God's gift, for by Him all things were made. In its more superficial layers of structure it is man-made, or rather man-assembled, the product of human labor and skill. It is the bearer of social and industrial life. If one were to bend an imaginative ear one could hear in this wafer the sound of plow, of tractor, of reaper, of mill, of train wheels, the hiss of gas within the baking oven, the clink of coins in the market.

Native to the thought of our brethren of the Eastern Church, pervaded here with the thought-forms of Platonism, this bread, brought into the arcana of the Church at the Great Entrance, is already holy, the representative of the Divine Logos by whom all things were made. Within the Parmenidean structure of this type of thought, inherited by Platonism, there is only being, never becoming, and therefore the bread offered in the Eucharist is the Logos as found in the nature of the earth, the sun, and the rain which He has made.

In our Western thought, dominated in these matters of philosophical distinction more by Aristotle than Plato, this is not so. This bread at the Offertory is but potentially holy, not actually holy. This is far more than a philosophical difference between potentiality and act; it is the fruit of divergent interpretations of the real.

Looking upon this bread as it is laid upon the altar we see it as God's gift, but the creative gift has been fabricated by man and therefore is unfinished, imperfect, and potential. This difference of view goes further than philosophical and theological divergence. To the Eastern mind, the elements when brought to the altar are caught up into an eschatological universe of perfection. To the Western priest, with his mind drenched by the philosophy of potentiality, the bread is but a man-made token of imperfection brought to God in penitence that it might be made holy.

In the Western view, the bread is not only a token of man's labor, but also of his sin. What he brings to God's altar is not only what we have wrought, but what has been left undone, and what has been done perversely and uncreatively. The bread is mildewed and stained. It is stained with our social injustice, our fratricidal wars. We have made bad bread. The tears of the oppressed, the twistedness of our hates, the envy, greed, pride, and lust of men have entered the bread. We have twisted the creative, existential energy of God into sin. This bread is symbolic of that twist and warp.

It is only, then, as this bread is broken in memory of the Atonement, and as it is offered in the name of the healing and sacrificial merit of our Lord, that it is worthy to be offered in thanksgiving to God. We make oblation at the Offertory, but we make Eucharist in the Consecration. There are two oblations in our rite, one the offering of what we have made out of God's created order, the second the offering of these gifts as they have been transformed by Incarnate and Atoning redemption. One is the offering of nature fabricated by man, the other the offering of Grace as given by God himself.

Man labors in the earth to make bread but because of his sinfulness the things he makes and does are marred. Only by the grace given to us by our Lord Jesus Christ can good bread be made.

The implications are obvious. As bread is used in the Eucharist, that is, as it is offered to God, in peace, in brotherhood, and in justice, and used for the physical and spiritual needs of men, so it must be made in the industrial and social order. Bread is to be grown, harvested, milled, baked, transported, and sold in justice and in love.

VI

THE EUCHARIST AND CHRISTIAN VOCATION

I have said that the Eucharist is not separate from life but is an intensification of its labor and its true nature. The

Eucharist points to a human society dealing with nature in justice and love. The mediating factor in this transformation of human society into a Eucharistic society is Christian vocation. There can be no other way by which what is seen to be true at the altar can be mediated into secular society. As men deal with bread in the Eucharist, so they must deal with it in the world. As men deal with bread on Sunday, so it must be dealt with on the other days of the week. And bread, of course, is the symbol of man's life, it is therefore any usufruct; it is iron, and coal and oil, and any other thing of nature which man deals with. We have said that the Eucharist is an intensification of the Eucharistic life, the life of making and distributing of things drawn from creative nature. The Eucharist is thus celebrated at every moment and at every hour. It is celebrated as we go forth from God's altar to do our work in the world. Mankind in general is the priest of God at the Eucharistic altar of the world. That altar is desk, bench, plow, and forge. It is thus through the vocation of Christian men sensitive of their Christian duty to produce, distribute, and consume in justice and peace, that the Eucharistic ethic, which is the Christian ethic of distributive and commutative justice, is implemented in action and in relationships in the world. Thus in the relationships of management and labor, in the honesty of advertiser and distributor with consumer, the Eucharistic action of bringing bread to God's altar is consummated in industrial and commercial life in the world.

The blessing at the close of our American Prayer Book rite often seems like a narcotic: 'The Peace of God!' Ought that to be the seemingly unchallenging and undemanding note with which we send forth our people into the world to fulfill their vocation? Bugles and battle cries would seem a better ending to a liturgy that does not end at the altar but in the world. For a Christian there can be no peace, no tranquility of soul, as long as social injustice exists in the world, and there is fratricide and hate on earth. 'The Peace of God' is, however, what we are sent forth to bring about and to make regnant, as members of Christ's Body that healed and restored in its incarnate existence in Galilee. We are the hands and feet, and the mouth of Him who brought both peace and a sword, the peace of healing and the sword of battling for righteousness. 'The Peace of God' then, may be, if rightly understood, not so much a narcotic as a commandment and a challenge. There is a vocation for everyone of us to work for justice and for peace. We are sent forth to make bread for nourishment and to make wine for joy. As these elements are dealt with at the altar, in brotherhood, justice, and peace, so may they by God's grace be dealt with in the world.

VII

SUMMARY

In summary, then, the Eucharist, by its intrinsic nature, implies the basic principle of the Christian philosophy of social relations, namely, that man is a social creature who is not merely social, but chiefly a person. Society exists to flower into persons. Man is neither a tool of the State nor of industry. He is not a tool like a drill press.

Secondly, the liturgy implies that industrial creation of artifacts are to be made and bought and advertised and financed according to principles of Christian brotherhood and love. Needless to say, love is not to be left as a vague, ethereal diffusion of attitude, but is to be rationally channeled into distributive and commutative justice. Justice is the matter of which love is the form.

Thirdly, the Eucharist implies the conservation of natural resources, that is, stewardship of and reverence toward God's gift of nature.

Fourthly, the Eucharist implies that as Holy Bread is made at the altar in brotherhood and peace, so daily bread must also be made in the world.

The bread which nourishes us is everywhere, both at altar and board, holy food.

V

THE LITURGICAL MOVEMENT
AND THE MINISTRY OF THE LAITY

Frank Stephen Cellier, Ph.D., L.H.D.

*Producer of Informational Programs,
Sears, Roebuck and Co.*

THE LITURGICAL MOVEMENT
AND THE MINISTRY OF THE LAITY

IN this paper[1] I shall use a number of Greek words over against their customary English equivalents. Perhaps it will be useful if I set these forth right away:

Over against 'Church,' I shall put *Ecclesia*; over against 'Gospel,' *Kerygma*; over against 'Worship,' *Leiturgia*; and over against 'Ministry,' *Diakonia*. The reason for this becomes quite clear, when one considers the numerous semantic overtones with which the words 'Church,' 'Gospel,' 'Worship,' and 'Ministry' are burdened,—or 'loaded,' if you will. 'Church,' for example, means many things to many people—often quite different and even incompatible things. The same can be said for the words 'Gospel,' 'Worship,' and 'Ministry.' So I hope I may settle, by contrast, for *Ecclesia, Kerygma, Leiturgia,* and *Diakonia.* These four words are the headings of the four sections into which I shall divide this paper.

---

[1] In preparing this paper, I have drawn on the researches and the insights of a great many people. I have drawn freely—to mention only a few—from Massey Shepherd, Arthur Lichtenberger, Stephen Bayne, William Temple, Hendrik Kraemer, Alan Richardson, William Nicholls, J. H. Oldham, and many others—last but not least among whom I would count one Saul of Tarsus, who under the name of Paul adventured himself into the theater (Acts 19:31) over and over again to the inestimable benefit of the *Ecclesia,* the Body of Christ, visible here in earth.

I should also point out that the words 'ecclesiastical' and 'sacerdotal' will be used deliberately in a contrasting sense. 'Ecclesiastical' will apply to the Church as a whole, the *Ecclesia,* the entire Body of them that are the 'called' according to His purpose (Rom. 8:28). 'Sacerdotal' will apply to the official, and unofficial, hierarchy of the empirical Church.

Finally, on the subject of vocabulary, the word 'World' will be frequently used, though in no single instance in a derogatory sense. It will be used to connote that which is not of the *Ecclesia.*

One last word by way of introduction: The Liturgical Movement is an earnest of the contemporary Reformation. This Reformation in our very own day is far less dramatic than the one of the sixteenth century. No one is going around tacking ninety-five theses on church doors, for example, in Wittenberg or anywhere else. But this twentieth-century Reformation is a profound and Church-shaking event, nonetheless. It has to do with the renewal of the Church, a re-understanding of its mission in the world. Of this significance of the Liturgical Movement, few are yet aware.[2]

Among clergy and laymen alike there is considerable confusion, if not sheer ignorance, about the Liturgical Movement. In extreme Evangelical circles the Movement is suspected of somehow being a lineal descendant of Oxford. In extreme Catholic circles the Movement is suspected of somehow wanting to tamper with the Victorian Eucharist. The Evangelicals happen to be wrong. The Catholics happen to be closer to the truth of the matter.

[2] See the papers of the Liturgical Conference held in Madison in May 1958: *The Liturgical Renewal of the Church,* edited by Massey H. Shepherd, Jr. (Oxford University Press, 1960).

The Liturgical Movement *is* tampering with the alleged Victorian 'splendor' of the Eucharist. In fact, the men of the Liturgical Movement go a great deal further. They are actually tampering with the medieval accretions to the Eucharist, particularly in the Latin rite, and its self-conscious imitators.

What many Anglicans simply do not know is that the Liturgical Movement originated nowhere else than in the Church of Rome. It has nothing whatever to do with, say, Phillips Brooks! It began with the rediscovery of the Gregorian chant in a reconstituted Roman abbey in France more than a century and a quarter ago. What Dom Guéranger and his monks in the French Abbey of Solesmes did for the liturgical chant was superb. However, he and they were typical products of the age of Romanticism in which they lived, and were simply not capable of applying the techniques of research scholarship to the task of recovering the full patristic liturgical heritage of the Church.

After the age of Romanticism had been suitably laid to rest, this task was, however, performed magnificently in the Roman Abbey of Maria Laach. While Solesmes had been concerned primarily with *form*, Maria Laach was concerned primarily with *substance*. Articulating the substance of Christian worship was the one great contribution of Maria Laach through its several publications, such as *Ecclesia Orans* and the *Jahrbuch für Liturgiewissenschaft*. Dom Odo Casel was the theological giant of this abbey. It was he who was primarily responsible for the reformulation of the ancient doctrine of Mystery Theology (*Mysterientheologie*). What Maria Laach set out to do, and what the contemporary Liturgical Movement in all Communions seeks to do today, is to recover the original status and function of the *Ecclesia*.

I

ECCLESIA

Let us ask first, what is the *Ecclesia*? It is, by derivation of the very word itself, 'them that are called out'—out of this world. The Christian *Ecclesia* began at Pentecost. Until that profound day had fully come, and they were all with one accord in one place (Acts 2:1), there was no Christian Church, no assembly of the Called Ones, the *Ecclesia*. The original Christian *Ecclesia* was the redeemed community—or, better, the community that understood the nature of man and the possibility of his redemption. It was the mystical Body of Christ. It was the new people of God. It was a fellowship (*koinonia*) of persons subpoenaed by God—

'Called' as St. Paul was called to be an apostle of Jesus Christ to the Gentiles (Rom. 1:1; I Cor. 1:1).

'Called' as were St. Peter's chosen generation, the royal priesthood, the holy nation, the peculiar people—to 'show forth the praises of him who hath called you out of darkness into his marvellous light' (I Pet. 2:9).

'Called' of Jesus Christ, as were 'all that be in Rome, beloved of God, called to be saints' (Rom. 1:6–7)—which is to say, Christians who live their lives in a mature knowledge of the faith; or 'adult Christians,' as Hendrik Kraemer puts it.

Perhaps one can most strongly emphasize the 'called' nature of the *Ecclesia* by pointing out what it is not. It is not, for example, representative of what Canon Wedel has labeled the 'Christianity of Main Street.' Neither is it a community whose God is, in Bishop Bayne's word, 'optional.'

I happen to know a publisher of some note who is not only non-Christian, but adamantly insists on calling himself anti-

Christian. His employees are very fond of him, not only because he is a very personable fellow, but also because his employment policies are just and even generous. He puts out printed material that you and I would find interesting, and no ladies' aid society could possibly object to. He does not, to the best of my knowledge, beat his wife. He houses and clothes and feeds his children better than well. He is a keen supporter of the United Fund in his community, and of the Boy Scouts.

Yet he is an anti-Christian. I repeat this in order to emphasize the fact that 'after all these things do the Gentiles seek' (Matt. 6:32). We Christians have no monopoly on being nice to people, loving our families, and being community-minded. You and I know hundreds and thousands of nominal Christians among both clergy and laity, between whom and my publisher friend the only difference is that he states his position more honestly.

What then is the difference between the Christian and the non-Christian? At this stage of our discussion, let us content ourselves by saying very simply that my friend the publisher is *man-minded*—period. The Christian, on the other hand, *minds men in Christ.*

This takes me back to the first speech of any consequence that I can ever remember making. It was a commencement address which I called 'The Household of Faith.' In this fresh-out-of-graduate-school protestation of mine, I held that the Faith in question was our faith in democracy. I spoke of a great democratic crescent with one of its horns set in the Nordic countries, its arc sweeping through the Western world, and its other horn implanted in the Antipodes. Fine prose, I thought, but absolute nonsense, of course, God forgive me. St. Paul's 'household of faith' has less than nothing to do with a political system loosely called 'democracy.' It has to do, instead, with the very opposite of the *kratein* of the *demos*—'the rule of the people.' It has to do with the *kratein* of *Christos*—'the rule of Christ.' The household of faith is, to sum it up, Christocratic, not democratic.

Obedience to God, in the terms of its Christocracy is, therefore, an *esse* of the *Ecclesia*, not merely a *bene esse*. Obedience to God is a primary and paramount note, without which the Church becomes a whited sepulchre, which indeed appears beautiful outwardly, but is 'within full of dead men's bones, and of all uncleanness' (Matt. 23:27). It is a note which far exceeds the other notes in importance—particularly those which enshrine the institutional sanctity of the empirical Church. The *Ecclesia* is the *Ecclesia* when its direction is Godwardly, when it 'implements' (as we say) the Lordship of Christ.

The Lord Christ not only called the first members of the Ecclesia, saying, 'Follow me!' (Matt. 4:19). He next *sent* them. The *Ecclesia*, historically—(and this is how we know the *Ecclesia* and can testify to it: historically)—was first called and then sent: 'Go ye therefore and teach all nations' (Matt. 28:19) . . . 'Ye shall be witnesses unto me both in Jerusalem, and in all Judaea and in Samaria, and unto the uttermost part of the earth' (Acts 1:8). As Kraemer puts it, the *Ecclesia* from the beginning was a body 'under marching orders.'[3]

The *Ecclesia*, whenever it has been faithful to the command of its Lord and Saviour, has been in a state of mission. The *Ecclesia* in its state of mission can well be compared to a traveler. A traveler is, by definition, a traveler for only as long as he travels. When he stops traveling and settles down, he ceases to be a traveler. In this sense, the Samaritan as he

---

[3] H. Kraemer, *A Theology of the Laity* (Westminster Press, 1958), p. 125.

journeyed (Luke 10:33–36) is a type of the *Ecclesia*: 'And on the morrow when he departed, he took out two pence, and gave them to the host, and said unto him, Take care of him; and whatsoever thou spendest more, when I come again, I will repay thee.' It was as he traveled that the Samaritan was neighbor unto him that fell among the thieves.

The *Ecclesia*, in the times of its purest Christianity, has dedicated itself to its kerygmatic mission—its mission to the non-Christian world with which it felt itself in constant tension. One reason for the empirical Church's softness today is precisely that it frequently fails to perceive the tension which always and inevitably exists between *Ecclesia* and World. The present-day Church exists in what Bishop Bayne has called a 'post-Christian' world. We are in urgent need of an ecclesiology which will take the realities of this post-Christian world into account. At the very least, such an ecclesiology will have to affirm that the *Ecclesia* has a kerygmatic mission to an alien society.

This ecclesiology will need to point up the twofold nature of the Church. First, it is an *institution*; and second, it performs a *function*.

There is no question about the necessity for its being an institution. The *Ecclesia* needs the organization of the Church. There have to be rectors, vestries, bishops, standing committees, wardens, altar guilds, men's clubs—or at least their equivalents. But the Church's primary reason for being is not to perpetuate these organizationalities. Its primary reason for being is that at its heart lies the *Ecclesia* with a function to perform in this world.

And the *Ecclesia* can perform this function, this kerygmatic mission, only through its members, the members of the Body of Christ. This means all of us: clergy and laity. We are, all of us, on mission. It is only as the Church is the *Ecclesia*—

that is to say, in a state of mission—that it is, in fact, the Church. To far too many people, the word 'Church' connotes a place, instead of men and women on mission. To far too many Church people, the word 'mission' still connotes dark Africa and yellow Asia. The Liturgical Movement is trying to teach us that 'mission' connotes *my* parish, *my* town, *my* city, right here and right now.

The men and women of the *Ecclesia*-on-mission consist of four orders. There are *four* orders of the Ministry, not three. The empirical Church, however, customarily restricts the terms 'minister' and 'ministry' to the ordained clergy. This usage inevitably sets the clergy in a class over against the laity. Our own Prayer Book is shot through with this usage. In our Eucharistic Prayer for the Whole State of Christ's Church, for example, we ask God to give His grace to Bishops and other Ministers that they may rightly and duly administer His holy Sacraments. It is far more accurate, and, in fact, indispensable to a satisfactory ecclesiology, to describe everybody in the *Ecclesia* as belonging to any one of the *four* orders of the Ministry—some deacons, some priests, some bishops, some laymen. I suggest to you that our current ecclesiology, with its sonic barrier between the first three orders and the fourth precludes, in practice, an effective statement of the ministry of the laity.

II

KERYGMA

For centuries the Church has fostered the assumption that retirement from the world is more 'Christian' than involvement in the world. In this connection, the Church has stressed the superiority of celibacy over marriage, the monastic priest over the secular, the clergyman over the man of affairs.

And yet, who of the *Ecclesia* is it, precisely, who is in a position to go and teach all nations (Matt. 28:19) and to be a witness (beginning at home) unto the uttermost part of the earth (Acts 1:8)? The *Ecclesia* exists for the very purpose of proclaiming, as we have said. It is to proclaim the good news: that the man who cannot obey the law is yet redeemable—or, better, is already redeemed. The *Ecclesia*, by its very nature, exists to proclaim this glorious redemption of the world. It is to interpret the mighty acts of God. It is to bring health to sick people the world over. It must face the fact that the world is sick. Today, as always, 'there is no health within us.' This is true no matter who we are or where we live. The world has probably never been in more desperate need of healing. And it is precisely when Christians are at large, when they are right in every nook and cranny of the world that they can be agents of this healing.

This is why we might well talk about the *diaspora* (dispersion) of the Church. When Christians disperse from the church building into the world, they are, in plain fact, the *Ecclesia*, scattered unto Jerusalem and Samaria and the uttermost part of the earth. On Sundays (and some weekdays, too) they re-assemble for basically two reasons: first, to receive the Body and Blood of Christ who renews the power of His Comforter within them; and second, to gain strength through their sheer *koinonia* or sense of belonging to one another, in Jesus Christ.

Now these Christians of the *diaspora*, these people who first gather in the church building, and then disperse into the world, and then gather again, are, of course, both clergy and laity, but primarily the laity. It is the laity who are in the world constantly. This in fact defines them: they are always in the world, but not of it. It is they who, just like the clergy, must proclaim the good news in all its fullness, wherever they find themselves.

The *laos* (people) of God are all four orders. Upon ordination the clergyman does not cease to be a layman. He remains, forever, one of the *laos,* the chosen people of God. And the *laos* must, in Archbishop Temple's words, insist on all those truths from which the distinctive quality of the *Ecclesia* is derived:

That God is Creator; and that man, with the world, is His creature;

that man has usurped the place of God in an endeavour to order his own life after his own will;

that in the Birth, Life, Death, Resurrection, and Ascension of Jesus Christ, God has Himself taken action for the redemption of mankind;

that in the Holy Spirit given by the Father through the Son to those who respond to the Gospel, power is offered for a life of obedience to God which is otherwise impossible for men;

that those who are thus empowered by the Spirit are a fellowship of the Spirit, or household of the Lord, fitly called the *Ecclesia*;

that in the *Ecclesia* are appointed means whereby men may receive and perpetually renew their union with their Lord and with one another in Him, and so increase in the Holy Spirit.

All this must be maintained and proclaimed, says Dr. Temple. And unless the *Ecclesia* is firm in its witness to its own faith, it will have no standing ground from which to address the world.[4]

I should like to put it clearly: Do our clergy and our laity in actual fact and in actual practice think of these great Christian affirmations as the *sine qua non* of our kerygmatic obligation to the world? To simplify—do we recognize that we are not the *Ecclesia* unless we affirm kerygmatically:

that first, man has usurped the place of God and wants to order his own life after his own will;

and that second, man can, nevertheless, renew his union with God through the Lord Christ, increasing in the Holy Spirit, and thus can achieve a life of obedience to God, which is otherwise impossible?

Let me say it this way: Are we for Christocracy first, or for Democracy?

To what extent do our words and our deeds proclaim the Lordship of Christ? To what extent does our *Kerygma*, our proclamation, hold the rule of Christ to be of the *esse* of the empirical Church rather than the rule of men? Our patristic forebears in the *Ecclesia*, of course, simply took it as given that the dominion was of Christ. Christocracy was their way of life. Pagan Greece had flirted with the notion that the dominion was not of God (nor of His *Logos*), but of man— hence Greek democracy. The eighteenth century (God save its naïve heart) lapped this up, and produced the blasphemous rationalism it is noted for. Where does the Church stand today? I know, and you know, where the *Ecclesia*

---

[4] William Temple, *What Christians Stand for in the Secular World* (Cincinnati: Forward Movement Publications), pp. 4–5. I have altered Dr. Temple's 'Church' to *Ecclesia*.

stands. But where does the *Church* stand? Is it for Christocracy or for Democracy?

I will say that the proclamation of the vast majority of our
laymen (I will not presume to speak for the clergy) is Democratic rather than Christo-cratic. It is, in other words, man-
centered, rather than God-centered. Being a Christian, they
say, is doing unto others as you would be done by. And this—
this doing unto others—they will say, one does of one's self.
One relies on one's own inner resources. This, they will say
further, is what is meant by man's being created in the image
of God.

This, of course, is Pelagianism, the only really 'damnable
heresy,' as Archbishop Temple called it. It is, at the same
time, the heresy which is the supreme characteristic of our
contemporary secular Anglo-Saxon society. As Bishop Wand
of London remarked, where could Pelagius possibly have
come from than from England?

And yet it is precisely our own Prayer Book which reminds
us constantly of the disastrous fallacy of human self-suf-
ficiency. Collect after Collect reiterates that 'we have no
power of ourselves to help ourselves,' that 'we cannot do
anything that is good without thee,' that without God 'nothing is strong, nothing is holy.' In our Collects, particularly,
we confess that 'without thee we are unable to please thee,'
and consequently we beseech God to prevent and follow us
with His grace, mercifully to grant that His 'Holy Spirit may
in all things direct and rule our hearts,' and to stir up our
wills that we might 'plenteously bring forth the fruit of good
works.'

The story is told[5] of the Episcopalian who arrived at the

---

[5] I give credit for this story to George Tittmann, Rector of the Church
of the Holy Spirit, Lake Forest, Illinois, and author of the unusually
perceptive book, *What Manner of Love* (Morehouse, 1959).

famed pearly gates and was informed by St. Peter that one needed 2000 points to enter.

'Tell me about yourself,' said St. Peter, making with the keys.

'Well,' said the Episcopalian, 'first I was baptized, then I was confirmed, and I always attended church regularly on Sundays, just like it says in the Prayer Book.'

'Good,' said St. Peter, 'one point. Anything else?'

'Why, yes,' the Episcopalian replied, 'I was also a Vestry-man in my parish for the maximum term—six years, I believe.'

'Fine,' said St. Peter, 'one more point. Anything else?'

'Why, of course,' replied the Episcopalian, a little bit ag-gressively, 'I was treasurer of our parish for many years, and the church never lost a cent during this time. We even paid all our bills!'

'Excellent,' said St. Peter, 'that's one more point. You now have three altogether. Anything else?'

'Well, at this rate,' said the Episcopalian, 'nothing will get me into heaven but the grace of God.'

'At last,' said St. Peter, '*that* counts for 1997 points. Now your total is 2000. Would you like to come in?'

In 1909, President Eliot of Harvard addressed his Divinity School on the subject of what he called 'modern true be-lievers.' They were, he said, those who 'contend against the sources of such misery by providing public baths, play-grounds, wider and cleaner streets, better dwellings, and more effective schools.'[6] At this point, I wish I had T. S. Eliot's chorus of the Canterbury women:

> after all these things do the Gentiles seek;
> after all these things do the Gentiles seek.

[6] Nathan M. Pusey, "A Religion for Now," *Harper's Magazine* Vol. 207, No. 1243 (December 1953), p. 20.

In commenting upon this address, President Pusey of Harvard said to the same Divinity School, that the enemies of President Eliot's 'true faith' were 'churches, creeds, priests, anything supernatural, any concern for a life after death, anything that professed to be sacramental.' These things, Dr. Pusey pointed out, Eliot 'would have considered . . . as so much twaddle.'[7]

What President Eliot did not, or probably could not, recognize is the fact that the *Ecclesia's* principal preoccupation is not with 'doing' but with 'being.' It is concerned primarily with what I *am,* and only secondarily with what I *do.* Realizing the truth of this rather elementary fact about the *Ecclesia* comes hard to most of us who have been reared in the stark and lonely and impoverished tradition of New England Puritanism. This Puritanism, with its bleak and untutored outlook on God and His creation, has been the very bane of the existence of the Holy Catholic Church upon this continent.

Empirical Puritanism, like empirical Romanism, has failed to put its finger on the signal difference between the Christian and the world. Fred Putnam, recently Rector of St. Matthew's, Evanston (now of St. James's, Wichita), put his finger on one of these differences. In the 'Rector's Corner' of the St. Matthew's weekly *Messenger,* Father Putnam wrote recently:

To be a Christian is to be different, and one of the great differences is the Christian's attitude toward his enemies and his opposition. A Christian need never be soft or stupid, foolish or naïve. A Christian is familiar with evil and he expects it in other people because he is aware of it in his own self. He differs from other people in the way that he deals with it. As St. Peter says: 'Do not return evil for evil or reviling for reviling; but on the contrary, bless.'

7 *Ibid.*

III
LEITURGIA

If Pelagianism is primarily occupied with *doing*, the *Ecclesia* is primarily occupied with *being*. While this fact is one of the most elementary fundamentals of theology, it is very largely unknown to the laity of the Christian world, Roman or non-Roman. It is highly doubtful whether the typical vestryman would even understand the statement that his ministry is primarily to *be*, and only secondarily to *do*. Rome, with its official emphasis on good works, and Protestantism with its unofficial emphasis on good works (in spite of its cardinal principle of Justification by Faith) are alike responsible for the contemporary layman's conception of Christianity as a 'religion of doing.' First, having; next, doing; and third, being—this is the order of values in our contemporary, post-Christian society. The order of the Church's classic understanding of the Faith is, of course, the reverse: first, being; next, doing; and then only (if at all), having.

The most fundamental question I can ask myself is, 'Who am I?' It is a question very few moderns ask. I suspect that most of the members of our congregations would not even know what the question means. And yet, before I can even begin to be a member of the *laos* in the *Ecclesia*, before I can begin to be a kerygmatic missioner, I must become profoundly aware that the most important fact of my entire existence is that I was lost—and am found; that I never stop trying to out-God God in my proud and arrogant knowledge of good and evil—and yet am redeemed; that I will kick against the pricks from here to Damascus—only to have the fact flash upon me over and over again that God is in Christ reconciling me, along with the rest of the world, to Himself (2 Cor. 5:19).

Once I understand what I am, once I know that without God I am unable to please God, I have no other option than to beseech God to prevent me in all my doings with His most gracious favor. And then, but only then, can what I proclaim be kerygmatic. By grace we are saved through faith. The works follow as summer does the spring. To place doing first, ahead of being, is, as we have said, sheer Pelagianism. And to place having ahead of both being and doing is, of course, blasphemous materialism.

But this blaspheming, materialistic society, relieved only by remnants of Pelagianism in most of the so-called Christian Churches, is precisely the society we live in. This is the alien, hostile, inimical world which the *Ecclesia* is sent to heal. These are our enemies from the fear of whom we pray God, in our Collect for Peace, to defend us.

It is not only ignorant, it is manifestly suicidal for the Church to ignore the deadly threat of contemporary secular society. The theology of Christ's Holy Catholic Church is surrounded and harassed, and constantly challenged to mortal combat, by the secular ideologies of our day—nationalism, racialism, individualism, materialism, communism. This ideological 'fall-out' has penetrated to the very bloodstream of the empirical Church, and accounts for the disease of 'ecclesiastical leukemia' that renders us so wretchedly weak when we should be about the business of buckling on the breastplate of faith (1 Thess. 5:8). Once we have addressed ourselves to the problem of being, we as the *Ecclesia* must address ourselves to the problem of doing. We are to teach, to baptize, and to minister (Matt. 28:19; Heb. 6:10).

But first we do have to be secure in our being; first we have to be 'persuaded that neither death nor life, nor angels, nor principalities, nor powers, nor things present, nor things to come, nor height, nor depth, nor anything else in all creation shall be able to separate us from the love of God, which is in Christ Jesus our Lord' (Rom. 8:38–39). Next, we will know that it is not we, but God who will, through us, set the world aright.

The *Ecclesia* can execute its healing mission only by the power of the Holy Spirit. As the apostles had to wait, after coming down from the mountain and praising God daily in the Temple, so we have to wait upon the ever-available blessing of Pentecost, for the Spirit of wisdom to come among us, and to fill us with truth and courage and the knowledge of God. The sublime author of the Acts of the Apostles reports the Lord Christ as saying at His Ascension, 'Ye shall receive power, after that the Holy Ghost is come upon you' (1:8). It was only after that momentous event that they were enabled to become witnesses unto Him, here, there, and everywhere, even unto the uttermost part of the earth.

There is one way and one way only for the Church to receive the power of the Holy Spirit, and this is by worshipping God. As Bishop Lichtenberger has put it, we must first say, 'Hallowed be thy Name,' in order that, subsequently, we may be in a position to say, 'Thy kingdom come.' First we must worship. After that, we may work for the spread of God's Kingdom.[8]

Our people need to understand more fully than they do in most parishes that they come to church in order to *perform* the liturgy, not to be spectators of it. What they come for is to let Christ in them offer themselves and their world to God, united with His own one, perfect, and sufficient sacrifice. As

[8] See his address "The Social Implications of the Liturgical Renewal," in Shepherd, *op. cit.*, p. 103.

Alfred Shands says, 'When the laity begin to realize that they are in part at least "co-consecrators" with the priest, they will be more ready to see Christ is the only true consecrator at the liturgy,' and that the priest will once again become the 'president' of the liturgical assembly.[9] This is heady talk—'co-consecrators with the priest'; the priest as 'the president of the liturgical assembly.' What would happen in the typical Episcopal parish if the laymen were to say to the Rector and his curates: 'You fellows are ministers of Christ, just as we are. We have talked some, about this profound responsibility, and have come to the conclusion that being is paramount to the Christian understanding, rather than doing—including even the thrill of setting up for the Christmas midnight Eucharist. What do you have to say to us about being?' The informed and dedicated laity of the Episcopal Church are standing right at this point. This is precisely the kind of question they are asking.

Where do the clergy, our Fathers-in-God, stand in respect to this? What leadership are they giving us? Is it not a pity that the first 'theology of the laity' in our day should have been written by a foreigner, a layman, a non-episcopally confirmed member of the Body of Christ?

Is it possible that we want it so? Is it possible that we are so preoccupied with the fourth point of the Quadrilateral that the only aspect of ministry, that is to say of *diakonia,* which we really care about is that our episcopally ordained priests should be suitably addressed? I ask these questions only because I want to ask an even more penetrating question. Is it an overstatement to say that while the *Ecclesia* has stood

---

[9] *The Liturgical Movement and the Local Church* (SCM Press, 1959), pp. 80–81.

under the perpetual subpoena of God, the empirical Church has all too frequently 'taken the Fifth'?

At this point, perhaps, I should draw attention to a remark by the Archbishop of York during his recent visit to our country. On being asked whether he had a word for the Church, he said, "yes—it would be Psalm 46, verse 10: 'Be still then, and know that I am God.' "

The way the *Ecclesia* at first, and always at its best, has worshipped is through the sacramental *mysterion* of the Holy Eucharist. In this sublime act, the Body of Christ becomes mystically identified with the Saviour Himself and unites its own self-giving with His one oblation of Himself once offered. It is only as we, the *Ecclesia*, identify ourselves with this ultimate sacrifice of Jesus Christ that our personal oblation takes on any meaning whatever. Our renewal of strength and power is found in the Eucharist. But our work is in the world—the whole complicated, diverse, wide world. It is wherever any one of us finds himself. It is in my office, on the plane, at my family dinner table, in bed with my wife, at my typewriter putting this paper together.

First, we say, 'Hallowed be thy Name,' and then we sacramentally receive the power to help make God's Kingdom come. First, we who are the *Ecclesia* perform the liturgy. Then, by God's grace, we live it.

Christians have a sacramental obligation toward their world. By the operation of the Holy Spirit within them, God's love flows through them into the world. The Christian, as a member of the royal priesthood, becomes a chosen channel of God's grace in his particular generation. And, as is perfectly obvious, no generation has more need of this sacramental benefit than our own, right here in the mid-twentieth century.

IV

DIAKONIA

Each one of us in the *Ecclesia* is a *diakonos*. This, by New Testament definition, is what all the *saints* are. They are *diakonoi*, ministers, called to a ministry, a *diakonia*, within and through the *Ecclesia*. St. Paul sets this forth with particular clarity in his letter to the Christians at Ephesus:

And he gave some, apostles; and some, prophets; and some, evangelists; and some, pastors and teachers; for the perfecting of the Christians to the work of *diakonia*, of ministry (4:11–12).[10]

St. Paul's *hagioi* means not just 'saints' as popularly understood, but all Christians. This is the way he generally salutes his churches: *hagioi*—saints—Christians—those of our fellowship. The Holy Ghost works, St. Paul is saying, in every one of us, collar or no collar, to perfect us Christians for the work of *diakonia*, of ministering, of service.

Pope Pius XII recognized this fact, at least in part. 'The laity,' he said, 'are the Church; they make the Church.' This statement is not to be interpreted too radically. Pope Pius, I am certain, hardly wanted to laicize his highly institutionalized and sacerdotalized Church. And yet, as Hendrik Kraemer points out, 'It is high time that the leadership of other churches showed the same clear-sightedness and determined action.'[11]

More than a century ago, Dr. Thomas Arnold put his finger on one of the reasons that there is such a difference between

---

[10] Cf. my translation with those of J. B. Phillips, Martin Luther, and the Dutch Reformed Church of South Africa.

[11] Op. cit. p. 72.

the empirical Church's understanding of ministry, and the *Ecclesia's* understanding of *diakonia*. Here is how Dr. Arnold put it: 'While the disciples of the Oxford Movement were rightly concerned with recovering a high doctrine of the Church, what they produced was a high doctrine of the ministry.'[12]

The word *laikos* in Greek, or *laicus* in Latin, has been bastardized from its original meaning. It has become a synonym for someone ignorant or even anti-Church. Actually, of course, *laikos*, from *laos*, has traditionally meant 'the chosen people of God.' It is interesting how the theological interpretation of the word *laikos* has paralleled the semantic. As the word went down in the linguistic class system, so did the concept go down in the theological class system.

The familiar dichotomies—spiritual and temporal, sacred and profane—are all features of what the Germans call the *Pastorenkirche* (Rectorial Church, Presbyterial Church, Sacerdotalized Church), the Church in which, in the words of Irenaeus, 'all the righteous possess the sacerdotal rank';[13] or, in the words of Ignatius and Cyprian, 'the Church is constituted by the bishop and his clergy.'[14] Our ecclesiastical vocabulary is shot through with this dualism: 'Holy Orders,' for example. The first three Orders are held to be holy. What of the fourth? What does our ecclesiology hold it to be? Unholy? Or in Britain, we have 'the Lords spiritual' and 'the Lords temporal.' What does our ecclesiology say of the Lords temporal throughout history? That they were invariably *pro-*

---

[12] Cited by Bishop Lichtenberger in Shepherd, op. cit. pp. 111–12.

[13] *Adv. haer,* iv. 8, 3.

[14] Cf. Ignatius *Phil.* 3, *Smyr.* 8; Cyprian *Ep.* lxviii. 8.

fane, and that the Lords spiritual were invariably *sacred* over the centuries, or are so in our own day?

There are not two kinds of Christians—higher and lower, spiritual and temporal, sacred and profane. I am quite convinced that St. Paul, for example, and St. Peter, too (not the Romanized St. Peter, but the one of the New Testament), would have been profoundly shocked by this kind of dichotomy. 'We, being many, are one body in Christ, and every one members one of another' (Rom. 12:5), St. Paul wrote to the Christians at Rome. And in his letter to the Corinthians, he said: 'The Churches of Asia salute you. Aquila and Priscilla salute you much in the Lord, with the church that is in their house. All the brethren greet you. Greet ye one another with an holy kiss' (1 Cor. 16:19–20). There is no class distinction here. Here there is no sacerdotal snobbery. These people are evidently convinced that they are one in the Lord, members of one Body, members of one another through Christ.

The *diakonia* clearly must be of the entire *Ecclesia,* clergy and laity alike. However, the trouble with us of the laity is that we are, to a large extent, spiritually illiterate. But whose fault is this? How consistently are you, Rectors of parishes, satisfied with a reasonably frequent attendance at the Eucharist, or, indeed, with the fact that your Vestry was amiable when you suggested alternating the Holy Eucharist with Morning Prayer at the main service on Sundays? What I am asking you is, I hope, clear: How consistently do you settle for institutional observance, at the price of functional action? Or, to use the vocabulary of this paper, what are you for basically: the empirical Church or the historical *Ecclesia?*

Let us face it. The laity is largely unequipped to function as *Ecclesia* in the world. The very men and women who come to communion faithfully, attend deanery meetings regularly, and even tithe year after year, are inarticulate and impotent in their kerygmatic obligation. They do not, most of them, even know that they have this obligation, let alone what to do with it. Who is to teach them? All of us, of course, all of us in the *Ecclesia*—clerical and lay members alike.

A young curate, one of my students at the seminary, said to me the other day that in an adult study group half of the class could not tell him which of the two Testaments was printed ahead of the other in the Bible.

The laity is in desperate need of being educated for what Dr. Kraemer calls 'a courageous and spiritually intelligent witness in the world.' We laity are confronting the clergy, our Fathers-in-God, with the stern and inexorable demand that they point the way for our *diakonia*, our ministry to the world. The clergy are to minister to the laity. The laity, primarily, is to minister to the world.

The laity confronts the clergy in this paramount matter with the same deadly seriousness that the layman, John Calvin, confronted the institutionalized clergy of his day. John Calvin's scholarship and John Calvin's Christian insight revolted against the clerical particularism of the sixteenth century. This is four hundred years later. And yet today, four hundred years later, the laity is still confronting the empirical Church with its same agonizing need to be taught how to speak a word of relevance to the world. The laity is restless.

The reason that laymen are best set to interpret the *Ecclesia* and its *Kerygma* to the world is precisely that they are *par excellence* the churchmen who spend their lives *in* the world. They know how the world thinks, talks, acts. They lunch with men of the world. They report to men of the world. Men of the world report to them.

The burning question which the Church must answer—and I do not mean the *Ecclesia,* but the Church in all the gorgeousness of its contemporary secular success—the question which the Church must face and answer is, therefore, simply this: Have we equipped the laity for witness? Have we rendered them articulate, convincedly articulate? Have we rendered them intelligent in the Faith? Do they know what they stand for, and can they say it and do it when they enter into discourse with the world? Today's layman faces an even more difficult challenge than the men and women whom St. Paul catalogues so conscientiously in epistle after epistle: 'Apostles, prophets, teachers, workers of miracles, gifts of healing, helps, governments, diversities of tongues' (cf. I Cor. 12:28–30).

The *Ecclesia* in the Western world functions in an atmosphere of amiable toleration. There is not really a tension, a struggle, going on. It is in the mission fields of Africa and Asia where the Christian religion encounters really respectable resistance. Here we are in direct encounter with an outspokenly alien and hostile ethos. And here, many churchmen are convinced, the *Ecclesia* bears its truest witness, as, for that matter, it did in Nazi Germany. It is here where the organizational and institutional divisions of Christianity lose all meaning. Here, even the fourth point of the Lambeth Quadrilateral begins to lose its meaning. The question is posed and deserves an answer—in terms of the *Ecclesia* confronting the Gentiles—is the fourth point of the Quadrilateral an *esse* of the *Ecclesia*, or is it merely a *bene esse*? Is it ecclesiastical or merely sacerdotal? Is it churchly or merely priestly?

It has been my high privilege to know many clergymen—bishops, priests, deacons, and plain 'ministers' (some Anglican, some not). My concern about them all is that they are necessarily preoccupied with the immediate problems of the organizational Church, that many of them falter in their vision of an *Ecclesia* with a *Kerygma* to the whole sorry world entire. And yet it is their task to tell themselves and their laity precisely this, that they, the laity, are the principal warhead on every missile which the *Ecclesia* lodges against the Prince of this world.

One can say with Congar, 'The laity are the new springtime of the Church.' But let us not be poetic about this. Let us look at it in pragmatic American terms. Let us not talk about babbling brooks and warbling birds. Let us talk instead about softness, and the mush, and the sickening sentimentality of what so often passes for Christianity. As *The Christian Century* pointed out in a recent editorial, 'the priesthood of all believers is going to have to be saved from some of the church's hugely successful men's organizations.'[15]

This reminds me of an incident in the experience of Dr. Walter Leibrecht, the Director of the Ecumenical Institute in Evanston. The men's club of a local church had invited him to give one of the season's three addresses designated as 'religious.' On arriving, he found the other two 'religious' speakers there also. Opening the meeting, the club's chairman explained everything: after the program had been sent to press, they had suddenly been lucky enough to add a wonderful magician and a lovely 'pop' singer to their year's program, so the three religious talks were being grouped into one single, great event!

But back to *The Christian Century* editorial. It goes on to say: 'This is the priesthood of all believers: every Christian, whoever or wherever he is, held to one standard of life and of knowledge, relating God's serious, gracious will to the world.' But, says the editorial, 'that is exactly what most of our laymen's organizations are not yet doing. . . . And when the

15 'No Pro-Tem Priesthood!' *The Christian Century* LXXV, 45 (Nov. 5, 1958), p. 1259.

men want to do something really Christian, they usually try to give the minister a hand—father's little helpers—so suggesting that the clergy is, after all, the real priesthood, and the way for the laity to get in on the act is to make like a minister, to be cut-rate reverends.'[16]

V

CONCLUSION

In sum, to live in the world as a member of the *Ecclesia*, one has to know what the *Ecclesia* is. In crass business terms, I can only 'sell' my product if I know it.

Our laity needs help, guidance—education, if you will. They need precisely the sort of counsel that the earliest Christians received in Corinth, or Galatia, or Rome, or Ephesus, when a letter arrived from Paul and was read, dissected, digested, and then proclaimed.

Of course, when you try to give them that kind of guidance, they will frequently say that they simply do not understand, that the material is too difficult for them. Yet for every one person who actually does understand something of what Christianity is all about, there are ten, or twenty, or thirty thousand who understand what *sports* are all about. For every one man in the Church who can speak an intelligible sentence about St. Paul's doctrine of Justification by Faith, there are tens of thousands who would be able to tell you that if Gerry Staley had not pitched a sinker in the bottom of the ninth in the last White Sox game against Cleveland, when

[16] Ibid.

Cleveland had only one man out and the bases loaded with the score 3 to 1 against them, and if Luis Apariccio had not caught that ball, tagged second, and then made the double play, the Sox might well have missed getting the pennant in 1959.

For every one man who can speak intelligently about Christianity, there are thousands who can speak with bewildering sophistication about baseball. This, it seems to me, leads to an inevitable conclusion: that those who are responsible for interpreting the *arena* are way ahead of us who are responsible for interpreting the *Ecclesia.* We need to catch up with the sports writers of America and become at the very least as effective as they are.

Our laity need to be informed in the Faith before they can exercise any *diakonia* whatever. They need to be taught what a life in dialogue with God is. A dialogue with God— that is what Dr. J. H. Oldham calls it in his brilliant study for the World Council of Churches. I can think of no fitter way of concluding this paper on the Ministry of the Laity than to quote a paragraph from Dr. Oldham's book:

The man, for whom life is a dialogue with God, is possessed of a fundamental humility. He knows that the best and highest human achievements are tainted with corruption. He is aware of his own finitude and the limitations of his own knowledge. He is consequently open-minded towards truth and tolerant of the views of others. He knows the folly of elevating any temporal end into an absolute, and is in consequence free from fanaticism. . . .

He is [also] free from anxiety about his immediate effectiveness, because his work is directed to a judgment beyond the flux of things. He knows that the results of men's actions very often prove to be quite different from, and even contrary to, what they intended, but this does not deter him from acting boldly because of his trust in God's forgiveness and His over-ruling and redeeming mercy.[17]

Let us put ourselves in a position to say to our laity in the words of Francis Ayres of Parishfield, with complete sincerity and with our Christian conscience clear:

> Go forth into the world as ministers of the living Christ,
>> to strengthen the weak,
>> to raise up those who fall,
>> to relieve the oppressed,
>> to preach the Gospel,
> to serve the Lord in the power of the Holy Spirit.

[17] J. H. Oldham, *Work in Modern Society* (Published for the Study Department, World Council of Churches, Morehouse-Gorham, 1950), pp. 37–8.

VI

THE LITURGICAL REVIVAL
AND THE ORTHODOX CHURCH

The Very Reverend Alexander Schmemann, S.T.D.

Professor of Church History and Liturgical Theology,
St. Vladimir's Orthodox Seminary

THE LITURGICAL REVIVAL
AND THE ORTHODOX CHURCH

SINCE the title of my address is somewhat ambiguous, I must define what I mean by 'The Liturgical Revival and the Orthodox Church.' Why was an Orthodox priest invited to speak at a Western liturgical conference, and in what capacity? There are many Orthodox who think that the Orthodox must always teach. Yet in my own studies in liturgics, I have found that much inspiration and many important insights have come from Western liturgical achievements. Therefore, it is not because of a 'secret' that we must proclaim and share with others that I am here.

It is true, however, that the Orthodox Church has always attracted the attention of all those who are active in matters liturgical. They have a natural sympathy for the East, and this for several reasons. Dom Olivier Rousseau, the Roman Catholic historian of the Liturgical Movement, wrote recently that the Eastern Church is the liturgical Church *par excellence*.[1] He even goes so far as to say that the Orthodox Church needs no liturgical revival because it has preserved intact the great liturgical prayer of the early Church. This, I think, is an overstatement. We all need a liturgical revival,

[1] *The Progress of the Liturgy* (Newman Press, 1951), pp. 139ff.

and the 'liturgical' Churches may be in need of it even more than the non-liturgical ones.

But it is true that the great names of St. Basil and St. John Chrysostom are not to be *discovered* in our tradition. They are there. Our liturgy is still deeply 'patristic,' and from this point of view the Western Liturgical Movement has been in many respects a *rediscovery* of some ideas and principles which in the Eastern tradition are 'natural.' Take, for example, Dom Odo Casel and some other leaders of the Liturgical Movement in Europe. They all attempt to rediscover the patristic idea of the liturgy and therefore are so deeply interested in the unbroken liturgical tradition of the Eastern Church.

There exist, of course, less valid reasons for this interest in the Eastern liturgy. Some people love it for its liturgical 'exoticism' and 'Orientalism,' for its being different from the Western patterns. This is, of course, a superficial approach. The real Liturgical Movement did not grow out of a 'rubricistic' curiosity or an interest in liturgical colors. It began with a strange shock experienced by some Christians when, after centuries and centuries, they realized of a sudden that Christ really said, 'Take, eat, this is my Body'—and it is not taken, not eaten. Or, as a Roman Catholic priest wrote, 'I was a priest for forty years before I knew what Easter meant in the life of the Church.' And this is why we all need a liturgical revival.

It so happened that in the West the liturgical revival was first of all a return to the *corporate* idea of worship. The underlying ecclesiological principle was that of the Church as the Body of Christ; and the whole movement took mainly that direction. And probably it is one of the most needed, most essential aspects and merits of the Liturgical Movement. But from the Orthodox point of view (and this is what justifies my appearance here), there are also other *dimensions* of the liturgy that must be rediscovered, brought back into our corporate experience of worship. To focus your attention on them is my purpose in this short paper.

At the beginning of my liturgical studies, I of necessity read the various theological and liturgical explanations of the Eucharist. I found that virtually all of them were *symbolical* explanations. Author after author, theologian after theologian, was making the same affirmation: that the Divine Liturgy is a *symbolical representation of the earthly life of Christ.* The Entrance with the Gospel, which we have at the beginning of the rite, 'represents' Christ going to preach, and the altar boy who precedes him with the candle is the 'symbol' of John the Baptist—and so on, through the whole service. If you take a Byzantine classic, Nicholas Cabasilas's Explanation of the Divine Liturgy, you will see that every detail of the service has a symbolical explanation, and sometimes not one but as many as four or five. Thus the exclamation: 'The doors, the doors!' can mean at the same time that the doors of our hearts must be closed to earthly temptations and open to the spiritual reality, or then that the doors of the Church are open to those who believe and closed to the heretics. But the partisans of 'symbolism' are never embarrassed by contradictions.

And yet, all theologians agree that within this 'symbolical' liturgy, at one precise moment, the 'symbolism' disappears and is replaced by 'realism.' When dealing with the transformation of the bread and wine into the Body and Blood of Christ, the term 'symbolical' is out of order and sounds heretical. We have thus a long 'symbolical' representation, one point of which and one point only ceases to be symbolical and becomes 'real presence.' And because of this, the theologians, leaving the symbolical framework to liturgiologists,

concentrate all their attention upon this precise moment, trying to define and to express its precision. *When* does it happen, *how* does it happen, and *what* exactly is it that happens?

The long controversies about the Eucharist were always
attempts to reach precise answers to these and similar questions. I am not quite certain that the type of precision
achieved in these elaborations is adequate to its object. But
it is clear that we have, as a result of it, two different ways of
looking at the Eucharist, ways which are by no means con-
nected with each other. The *liturgical* approach (in the old
acceptance of the term 'liturgical') is concerned with symbolism in all its possible variations. The *theological* approach
isolates the *quid* of the liturgy from its liturgical framework
(thought of as precisely a framework, useful and beautiful
but not essentially necessary), and deals exclusively with
the question of the *validity*: i.e. the minimum of conditions
required for the Eucharist. In my opinion, the time has come
for *liturgical theology*, or, in other terms, for a theology that
would respect the liturgy as we receive it from tradition, and
a liturgiology whose aim would once more be the formula-
tion and explication of the *lex orandi* as *lex credendi* of the
Church.

In this approach, the question, which for a long time has
been not only central but almost the only question in all
Eucharistic theology—namely, *what* happens to the elements
(and the *how* and the *when*)—must not precede, but must
follow another basic question. *What happens to the Church
in the Eucharist?* For it is only when this question is asked
that certain of the affirmations made by the Eastern Church
can be understood: The affirmation—for example, that the
very idea of a *moment* of consecration and also of the
essential and the *non-essential* acts in the liturgy, etc., are
not adequate—should not be applied in Eucharistic theology;

nor should the affirmation that it is the *Epiclesis,* the invocation of the Holy Spirit, that constitutes the real 'form' of the
Eucharistic sacrament. At the time they were made, they expressed the opposition of the Orthodox Church to some
Western theories rather than a consistent sacramental doctrine. But, as we move toward a liturgical theology, they
acquire their full meaning and become the starting points
of a fuller theological understanding of the Eucharist.

In this short presentation, I want to take you through a
quick analysis of the Eucharist, as it is celebrated in the
Orthodox Church. We know that the basic 'shape of the
liturgy,' to use the phrase of Gregory Dix, is common to all
liturgical traditions. The Byzantine liturgy, however—and
in spite of a certain enmity for it of the same Dom Dix—remains, in my opinion, a unique theological and liturgical
synthesis. It could perhaps be purified of certain elements,
introduced in it under the influence of the above-mentioned
symbolism, and also of some 'Orientalisms' (for one has to
distinguish between the 'Eastern' and the 'Oriental,' when
one deals with Orthodox worship). But even as it stands now
it is still the best and the fullest expression of Catholic worship. This is why I suggest that we analyze it briefly, and
perhaps some of the questions which I raised at the beginning
of this paper will at least receive a preliminary and tentative
answer.

Let me stress once more that the very spirit of liturgy, as
the Eastern Church understands it, excludes the distinction
between the 'important' and the 'unimportant' moments or
acts. To Orthodox young people who often ask me, 'Father,
what is the most important moment of the liturgy?,' I always
give the same answer: 'The whole liturgy.' And I add some
illustration such as this: 'When you want water to boil and
therefore consider that the important moment is when it

finally boils, you still know that you will not reach this point unless you first let the water warm up.' The Eucharist can be viewed as a journey or a *procession,* which leads us ultimately to the final destination, but in which every stage is equally important.

This procession actually begins when Christians leave their homes for the church. They leave their life in this present world, and whether they have to drive fifteen miles or just walk a few blocks, a *liturgical act* is already taking place, and this act is the very condition of everything else that is to happen. They are now on their way to *constitute the Church,* for their gathering together results not in a mere sum of so many individuals, but in the *ecclesia,* the Church. This is the first *transformation* that takes place at the Liturgy, and it is not a symbolical one. It is the first in a long sequence of transformations which altogether constitute the Liturgy, the Sacrament of the Church, its fulfillment.

The minister of this transformation, as well as of all the others, is the Priest. Without his coming, the group would remain just another human group and, however spiritual or even holy, not the Church. But the celebrant stands in the center, and his vestments and insignia express first of all and above everything else his relation to the body of the Church as its head: *totus Christus, caput et corpus.*

Then comes the initial acclamation: 'Blessed is the kingdom of the Father, the Son, and the Holy Spirit.' From the beginning the destination is announced: the journey is to the Kingdom. This is where we are going, and again—not symbolically, not psychologically—but indeed, really and 'ontologically.' The congregation answers *Amen*; and it is probably one of the most important liturgical terms, for it expresses the agreement of the Church to follow Christ in His Ascension to His Father.

During the first part of the Liturgy, the Bishop stands in the center of the church. He has not approached the altar. He has not entered the sanctuary. He is in the center of his flock—the Pastor, the leader, the head of the body. And the Liturgy begins by the common prayers and supplications of the assembly, a common and joyful praise. This joyful character of the Eucharistic gathering must be stressed. For the medieval emphasis on the Cross, the sacrificial character of the Eucharist, while not a wrong one, is certainly one-sided. The Liturgy is, first of all, the Paschal gathering of those who are to meet the risen Lord and to enter with Him in His Kingdom.

Then comes the *Entrance*. If, from its usual symbolical explanation, we go back to its real meaning, we discover that it is not a symbolical, but a *real* entrance. It is the real approaching of the altar, a real entrance into the sanctuary, which in liturgy *re-presents* (makes present) the Kingdom. It is the place of Divine Presence, the place where the Table of the Lord is being prepared for us, where once more we are invited to partake of the banquet of the Kingdom. It is therefore a solemn Entrance. And when the Bishop enters the Royal Door of the Iconostasis, in him we all, the whole body, perform the same entrance, for he is the head of the body.

At this point appears the liturgical theme of *Angels*, and we must consider it briefly. It is noteworthy that in the Byzantine liturgical synthesis the 'terms of reference' of the Entrance are precisely the angelic powers. We sing the angelic *Trisagion*: 'Holy God, Holy Mighty, Holy Immortal'; and the prayer which the priest reads after he has approached the altar begins by a mention of the angels ('O holy God . . . who art praised with thrice-holy voice of the Seraphim, glorified by the Cherubim, and adored by all hosts of heaven,' etc.).

The angels are not here for decoration, or because it is nice and inspiring to mention the Seraphim and the Cherubim from time to time. The liturgical function of this mention (and this also is true of the *Sanctus*) is to certify that the Church has entered its heavenly dimension, has *ascended into heaven*. It indicates that we are now at the Throne of God, where the angels eternally sing 'Holy, Holy, Holy.'

Thus, following the first step—our transformation into the Church—the Liturgy now has achieved its second step: the entrance into the *aion* to which the Church continually belongs. The priest, who now stands before the altar, says: 'O Holy God.' He gives God His *real* Name, and worship its real, heavenly essence, because 'holiness' means, on the one hand, that God is the Absolutely Other, and, on the other hand, that He is the desire of all our desire, the goal and fulfillment of our life. And then while the choir sings—slowly, solemnly—the *Trisagion* Hymn, the procession moves further. The celebrant goes behind the altar (the 'high place' or the 'throne' in Byzantine liturgical terminology) and, for the first time, turns back and faces the people. Now he himself is being transformed. For up to this moment he was the one who *led* the Church in its ascension to the heavenly altar; but when he turns now his face to the people and, raising his hand, says, 'Peace be with you all,' the movement has reached its goal and the Presence of God *given* us. He spoke *for* the Church, and now he speaks *to* the Church. He re-presented the Church before God, and now he re-presents God to the Church. And fulfilling thus his ministry, he re-presents Christ, the Head of the new humanity and the One who reveals God, the Emmanuel.

For a long time the movement of the Liturgy was explained as a movement *downwards*: as grace which the priest takes 'from heaven' and brings down to us. It seems to me that such an explanation must be completed by its opposite. It is not God who is being taken from heaven, placed on our altars, and then put into the mouths of men. It is the Church that is being lifted up and ascends to heaven. A very important liturgical category is that of Christ's Ascension, and we must not forget that the first manual of liturgics, the Epistle to the Hebrews, was written precisely in terms of Ascension.

The Entrance is thus the ascension of the Church to where it belongs. Although it is still in this *aion*, in this world and its time, it is essential for the Church to leave 'this world' and to recover regularly this dimension of Ascension; and this is done in and through the Liturgy. And it is in this dimension of the Kingdom that we listen again to the Word of God. In our Church, the Epistle is read by a layman, the Gospel by the deacon, and the Sermon is preached by the priest. All Orders of the Church take part in the 'liturgy of the Word,' the text of Scripture given to the whole Church. But it belongs to the priest to perform the Sacrament of the Word, and this is the real meaning of the *liturgical Sermon*. In it the 'text' (the human word of Scripture) is *transformed* into the Word of God to be given us. It was Origen who said that there were two communions at the Liturgy: the first, the Word of God; the second, the Body and Blood.

With the liturgical Sermon, the first part of the Liturgy—the *Synaxis*—comes to its end, and we move into the Eucharistic sacrifice. Much has been written about the sacrificial character of the Eucharist, yet the issue still remains confused. Perhaps a very simple liturgical approach can help here.

First, we offer to God some very simple elements of our food: some bread and some wine. As you probably know, the Eastern Church uses the leavened bread for its *prosphora*; so it is really what we eat at home that is being offered to God as our sacrifice. And a good liturgical and Biblical study would clearly show that this offering of food means, first of all, that we are *offering ourselves*. Food is not only the symbol of life, but being the condition of life, being that which becomes our body, food *is* life and therefore *our* life—we ourselves. The first and real sacrifice is, thus, the sacrifice of the Church itself. But (and this 'but' is very important) it is a *sacrifice in Christ*. It is not a new sacrifice because it is the sacrifice of the Church, and the Church is the Body of Christ. From the first moment of the Liturgy, Christ is not only the One who *accepts* the sacrifice, but, in the words of one of the liturgical prayers, the One who also *offers*. All our sacrifices—and a Christian is by his very nature a living sacrifice to God—converge at the one and unique sacrifice, full and perfect, that of Christ's humanity, which He offered to God and in which we are included through our membership in the Church.

We are offering this sacrifice not because God needs it, but because Christ's sacrifice is the essence, the condition of our being in Him. The Orthodox theology, when contemplating this sacrifice, stresses love in it rather than 'satisfaction' or expiation. To be a sacrificial Being belongs to the very essence of the Son of God even before Incarnation and Redemption. For *sacrifice*, before it becomes sacrifice for something, is the natural and necessary expression of love. Christ's whole life is a sacrifice because it is a perfect life made of love and love alone. And since it is His own life that He gives us (Christ in us, we in Christ) our life is also a sacrifice. Our sacrifice in Him, His sacrifice in us. And thus again, it is a real, not a symbolical sacrifice; yet not a new one, but always the same, the one that He gave us, into which He has taken us. The Church, being the Body of Christ, is itself a sacrificial being because it knows that the essence of man's life—as seen in His Humanity—is to *go to God*. And this going determines the movement of sacrifice. All this is expressed in the Prayer of the Cherubim Hymn: 'Thou art the One who offers and the One who art offered, and Thou receivest and Thou art distributed.'

It is a wonderful identification with Christ. We offer *our* sacrifice to God the Father, and yet we have nothing to offer but Christ Himself; for He is our life and offering. Sacrificing our life, we offer Him. Our Eucharist is His Eucharist, and He also *is* our Eucharist.

After the Creed and the Kiss of Love ('Let us love one another that in one accord we may confess,' etc.) we are ready for the great Eucharistic prayer, which from time immemorial constituted the very essence of the whole Eucharist. Eucharist means thanksgiving. *But how is thanksgiving related to consecration?* To this question the various theological theories give no satisfactory answer. Under their influence the thanksgiving element of the Eucharistic prayer was called *Preface.* Yet a preface is usually not something too important. Do we not sometimes read the preface of a book after we have read the book itself? But in the Eucharist it is precisely this 'Preface' that makes everything else, including the consecration and the transformation of the elements, possible; and we understand why thanksgiving is the *only* way to that transformation and so understand the whole meaning of the Eucharist.

For centuries the emphasis was laid on the 'night in which He was betrayed'—on the bloody aspect of His sacrifice. But in liturgical tradition, which no sacramental theory has been able to break, the prayer begins with a solemn thanksgiving. And Christ also began His sacrifice with a thanksgiving: 'And when He had given thanks, He broke it . . . and gave it.'

The reason for this, however, forgotten as it may be, is a simple one. Eucharist, thanksgiving, is the state of the innocent man, the state of paradise. Before sin, man's life was eucharistic, for 'eucharist' is the only relationship between God and man which transcends and transforms man's created condition. This condition is that of a total, an absolute dependence. Dependence is slavery. But when this dependence is accepted and lived as 'eucharist,' i.e. as love, thanksgiving, adoration, it is no longer dependence; it is an attitude of freedom, a state in which God is the *content* of life. Eucharist, thus, is the only state of innocence, and Adam and Eve had it and it was the divine image of them.

Then man lost it. There are many theories of what original sin was, but in terms of liturgical theology one can say that the original sin was the loss of that eucharistic state. The loss of the real life, which is eucharistic life, was the loss of life in love and communion. The Old Testament reflects an endless attempt to recover 'eucharist,' but no one can offer it fully because 'eucharist' is the state, the attitude, and the act of the innocent man in whom life, meaning of life, and fullness of life are one and the same thing. It was a certain experience of life that man had lost—the eucharistic experience. But then salvation could be nothing else but the restoration of life as 'eucharist.' It was restored in Christ. His whole life, and He Himself, was a perfect Eucharist, a full and perfect offering to God. Thus the Eucharist was restored to man.

Therefore, when the priest proclaims: 'Let us give thanks unto the Lord!'—we realize that the whole movement, the whole procession was necessary for it was achieving the state of innocence, making the Eucharist possible. And now once more man stands before God restored to his pristine beauty, innocent, perfect, the very image of God's love. He has nothing to ask for, for he has already received 'grace upon grace' and has been admitted to the Kingdom. What does then remain?

When the movement, the procession, reaches its goal, and all prayers have been said and everything that exists has been commemorated, there remains but one ultimate reality—the Eucharist. This is why the whole movement comes to this last and unique exhortation: *eucharistesomen* ('Let us give thanks!').

But we know that no one can say this, no one can offer this but Christ. It was His unique Eucharist that has led us up to this point; we were taken into His Ascension, His *passage* to His Father. We were offering in Him. And now we realize that the *content* of our Eucharist is Christ again, for there is nothing else that we can offer to God. It is not a new Eucharist. We are accepted into the eternal Eucharist which Christ offers and of which He is the offering. He stands there—in heaven—eternally. He is the end, the *Eschaton*, and our Eucharist is thus not in the past, the present, or the future. It is in the *Eschaton*, in the glorified Christ.

Now we can understand the relation between the Eucharist and the consecration. We can say that what 'happens' to the elements of bread and wine happens precisely because of our being in the Eucharist, in the *Eschaton*. It happens because we are in the *aion*, in which the transformation is not a mere 'miracle,' but somehow the natural consequence of our ascension into it. The food (the life!) which God gives us is once more He Himself.

Of this fulfillment of the Eucharistic procession, of our 'arrival' and acceptance in the Kingdom, the *Sanctus* is the expression and sign. We sing the angelic hymn because in Christ we have entered heaven. And having entered there, we offer Christ as our Eucharist, because 'by nature' we have

no admittance, because only in Him this has become possible.
Hence—the *Anamnesis,* the recapitulation of how all this
happened, of the whole economy of salvation. This is what
we 'remember' in heaven, before the throne of God, because
there is nothing else that man could remember and offer.

And then in this remembrance we come to that night, to
that Supper, and we repeat what He said then: 'Take, eat . . .
drink . . . do this.' Having reached this point, the movement
of the Eucharist is reversed. Until now, we were ascending,
going up, moving toward God. But now once more He comes
to us, as in Paradise, to feed us with the new life of the new
aion, to fulfill His communion with us. This moment of rever-
sion is the consecration. It is the sign that our offering has
been accepted, that our Eucharist has been fulfilled, that we
have entered into the eternal Eucharist of Jesus Christ.

The Orthodox Church has always affirmed the necessity of
the *Epiclesis,* the invocation of the Holy Spirit, for the consecration, i.e. the transformation of bread and wine into the
Body and Blood of Christ. This affirmation is still the object
of a heated controversy, both historical and theological. But
one has to go beyond the purely historical or purely scholastic
argumentation and discover the true significance of the Holy
Spirit in the Eucharist. His coming, His action, means always
the fulfillment of the *Eschaton,* the coming of the new *aion,*
the last Day. And in the Eucharist, which is the Sacrament of
the Church, the *Epiclesis* means that the ultimate transformation has become possible only because of our entrance in
heaven, our being in the *Eschaton,* in the day of Pentecost
which is the day after and beyond the seventh day, the day
which is beyond time, the day of the Spirit.

The last action of the Eucharist is the participation in the
eschatological banquet of the Kingdom, the communion. Its

importance has been duly stressed in the Liturgical Movement. But I must again and again point to its meaning as our participation in the *world to come*. It is our communion in the Spirit, or, in other terms, in the *aion* of the Kingdom.

Then the priest says: 'Let us depart in peace.' This does not mean, of course, that having accomplished our religious duty we can now simply go home and 'relax.' How can one *return* from the Kingdom? And yet we are given this order, and it is precisely as an order that those words must be understood. This gives the Eucharist its last dimension—that of *Mission*.

We were first ordered to leave the world and forget it: 'Let us put aside all earthly care.' And this was the condition of our ascension into the *Parousia*, the Presence of Christ, of our communion in the Spirit. But now that 'we have seen the true light and partaken of the Holy Spirit,' now that we have fully realized the Church as being not of this world, we are sent back in the world and the eschatological sacrament becomes the very condition of our work and life in it. For the sacrament has made us capable of bearing testimony to the Kingdom and life eternal. 'We have seen, we have touched, we have been *there* . . .' And we can thus be responsible Christians, for we can now refer everything to that which happened to us—to that eucharistic ascension on Mount Tabor. It is here that we find the guiding principle for our Christian action in the world. By transforming the Church into what it is, the Eucharist makes it capable of being the real center and heart of its mission to the world.

The Eucharist is thus the Sacrament of the Church, transforming us again and again into *membra Christi*. It is then the Sacrament of the real Sacrifice, in which our sacrifice becomes that of Christ. And it is finally the Sacrament of the

Parousia, the Presence of Christ and of His Kingdom. These three aspects of the Eucharist must be always kept together, and it is one of the main tasks of the Liturgical Movement to recover the eschatological dimension of the liturgy. The real life of the Church is revealed and fulfilled every Sunday. We partake of the *Eschaton* and to it we can witness in our life in this world. If we realize this, the Liturgical Movement acquires a real sense of purpose.

VII

THE EUCHARISTIC LIFE
A SERMON

The Right Reverend John Pares Craine, D.D.

Bishop of Indianapolis

THE EUCHARISTIC LIFE

A SERMON

THOUGHTFUL man must always know who he is and what his life represents. Even the most generous critic of the American scene today would scarcely dare to call this a thoughtful time. In a materialistic age, when we have almost come to worship our own productivity, we have also known our deepest anxieties in this same area. We are threatened by the possibility of another nation out-producing us scientifically, by the fear of loss of world markets, and—on the personal side—we are constantly under the stress of concern for our own competence in relation both to worldly success and to interpersonal relationships. In a secularistic period such as this, man is inclined to cease being thoughtful and reflective, to yield himself instead to emotional reactions of despair or elation, and to settle into the business of living with grim determination. As he loses confidence in his own institutions of business or politics or religion, he defends and attacks them equally with a stronger passion.

Into this world comes the Lord Jesus Christ eternally, to confront those who would listen and think and act with the only real choices of life.

He was in the world, and the world was made by him, and the world knew him not. He came unto his own, as his own received him not. But as many as received him, to them gave he power to become the sons of God, even to them that believe on his name: which were born, not of blood, nor of the will of the flesh, nor of the will of man, but of God. (John 1:10–13.)

'As many as received him . . . ' Scripture reminds us that such as believed in the Lord Jesus were added to the Church. The congregation of the faithful says this to the godparents, or to the person about to be baptized, in the declaration that they have prayed 'that our Lord Jesus Christ would vouchsafe to receive him.' There are those telling questions asked of the adult convert at Baptism: 'Dost thou believe in Jesus the Christ, the Son of the Living God?' and 'Dost thou accept him, and desire to follow him as thy Saviour and Lord?' And there is that key question asked of the candidates for Confirmation: 'Do you promise to follow Jesus Christ as your Lord and Saviour?' The Christian is the thoughtful man who has received the Lord Jesus Christ. Having received Him, he has thus received from Him the power to become a son of God.

Thus, as a thoughtful man, he knows who he is and what his life represents. First John (the Epistle for this week) reinforces this knowledge with the words: 'Behold, what manner of love the Father hath bestowed upon us, that we should be called the sons of God. . . . Beloved, now are we the sons of God, and it doth not yet appear what we shall be: but we know that, when he shall appear, we shall be like him; for we shall see him as he is.' (I John 3:1-2.) I know who I am only because I trust the Lord Jesus, and I know my life has significance only so long as I am obedient to Him; for truly my life is hid with Christ in God. The thoughtful Christian must know four facts irrevocably.

(1) The first fact he must know is that he is chosen for this

role. This is no self-seeking, no striving on his part for recognition or prestige. Not a one of you is here this day because you choose to be. You are here because you were chosen; you were ordained to be here. The choice of your presence here was made known to you through a variety of persons and circumstances. This is the way God works. Jesus said to His disciples: 'Ye have not chosen me, but I have chosen you, and ordained you.' (John 15:16.) I was born, 'not of blood, nor of the will of the flesh, nor of the will of man, but of God.' Therefore, my sole task is not to seek, but simply to obey.

What a load this lifts from us in the choices that confront us! All we have to do now is to recollect who we are, and why we were chosen, and what role God has for us to play. The roles of a bishop, a priest, a deacon, or a layman are all well documented in Christian history. We have only to study the part as it was played by the great artists down through the centuries, and learn to pattern our lives after the best examples of craftsmanship. This is only one part of the communion of saints—that we should have this help—but it is a blessed one.

Only in man, of all God's creation, does this problem of obedience lie. All of the rest of creation can only be what God intends it to be. A tree can be only a tree; a moose, a moose; and a mouse, a mouse. A tree cannot be a bird or an elk or a man. So it stands, as God made it, subject as we are to the storm, the blight, the drought, the soil conditions, the temperature, the fire, and the axe. But always it is obedient. And here is another lesson of this chosen-ness: it does not worry about its appearance, its importance, or its end. It is content to be. How often some poor soul says to us, 'I am not important. I do not count for anything. I will drop out.' Or, 'I am not good enough.' You long to have them understand you when you say that God chose them for a purpose, as He did with all His creation, and that He wants them now to be obedient and faithful to that choice.

Some people are confused about our Lord's injunction that we must be perfect. Because they do not have a voice like Caruso, or even like some of our choristers, they hold back and fail to use to the full the voice God gave them. When you have accepted the fact that you are chosen, you are no longer fearful of your limitations. You are not ashamed or afraid of who you are. You are not a result of a series of accidents, but of a series of choices. This is a supernatural choosing. You are grateful that God has seen fit to do you the supreme honor of choosing you. All you have to do is to accept the Lord Jesus Christ.

(2) The second fact the thoughtful man must know follows quite simply from the first. It is that he must know that obedience demands an immense faithfulness on his part. The Church does not leave him to his own devices in this, but provides him with a discipline under which he may learn the nature of his dignity and true freedom. This is the reason for the Church's being. As the Body of Christ, the Church provides a fellowship for nourishing and sustaining his life, and a vehicle for carrying on the mind and mission of Christ in this our generation. It spells out clearly the bounden duty of the Christian: 'to follow Christ, to worship God every Sunday in his Church; and to work and pray and give for the spread of his kingdom.'

Why a thoughtful man can ever take these duties lightly always escapes me. In a society which has so clearly emphasized the need of training and preparation for the performance of its tasks, it is incredible that anyone could believe that the spiritual life can be nurtured with any less discipline. Man cannot expect to learn God's will for him, nor be obedient to it, without this faithfulness to this simple discipline. It takes patient years to deepen and ripen this discipleship. Then, sometimes, it is only as we look back that we know we have been obedient. The Sunday by Sunday faithfulness, without question of the fidelity of others, without irritation at the human frailties of the priest, without measuring our success by the quality of our feelings of God's nearness, with fullest participation in the liturgy—these are the marks of that obedience. The Church's calendar and colors mark the change of the seasons; the years go by, and some days we have quite an awareness that the fruits of the Spirit are beginning to ripen in us.

A child can know fun and pleasure and excitement; only an adult can know the depths of joy. A child can know the spontaneous show of affection or gratitude; only a spiritually mature person can really know the full depth of a love which pours itself out to the beloved. A child can know instant satisfaction at the gratification of desires; only an adult can know the deep quiet of peace in the performance of duty. Love, joy, peace—the fruits of the Spirit—can only come to us through patient growth and faithfulness.

(3) The third fact the thoughtful man must know illustrates the curious alternation between God's part and man's part. This fact consists of the wonderful assistance God gives us through sacramental grace, which is known to us primarily through the Eucharist, in the congregation of the faithful. The institution of the Eucharist on the night before His crucifixion chronologically illustrates the fact that this Blessed Sacrament is the summary of His life and work. Here, all that Jesus is and does is gathered up and poured out for us. Here, we who have accepted Jesus Christ as our Lord and Saviour are made 'very members incorporate' in His mystical Body, 'the blessed company of all faithful people.' Here,

our sinful bodies are made clean by His Body, and our souls washed through His most precious Blood, 'that we may evermore dwell in Him, and He in us.'

Now we know who we are and why we are here. We are learning to acknowledge our manhood, made in the image of God, and in offering it thus to Him in the Eucharist, we are also learning to be grateful for who we are, instead of being so often distrustful, discouraged, or unmindful, as we are inclined to be. This is the nature of the Eucharist as an act of thanksgiving. This is also the nature of true freedom, a freedom from self-centeredness and self-concern. We are unaware of self, for it is Christ who works in us His good purposes. This is the summary of our life and work, as it is the summary of His. Here 'we offer and present ourselves, our souls and bodies, to be a reasonable, holy, and living sacrifice.' A sacrifice is a death, death unto self and life unto God through Jesus Christ our Lord. Our life is no old leaven, nor the leaven of malice and wickedness, but the unleavened bread of sincerity and truth. For this one glorious moment, we too are dead unto sin and alive unto God. He takes the bread of our life, mingled with the lives of the congregation of the faithful, and makes all the bread His own Body to be returned to us.

The Church does not exist to make men good, or healthy, or successful. It lives to communicate the life of God to His children. The Church is the Body of Christ, receiving and communicating that Body. It is the Bride of Christ, and lives out a love-song of pouring out its life and receiving His life. Goodness, health, love, joy, peace—all else follows from this communication of life. The Church is most perfectly the Church in the Eucharist. Just as the Cross summarizes all that Jesus came to do and to teach, so the Eucharist continues this life poured out through eternity, mediating life between man and God, redeeming life constantly. Life is more than flesh and blood; but life is communicated in the human world through Flesh and Blood. Truly the communion rail is the gate of heaven. Here God gives life and man may know who he is as he learns to offer himself. The great devotional literature of our Hymnal and the books and tracts on man's appreciation of the Blessed Sacrament through the centuries testify eloquently to these greatest moments of man's awareness of his place in the universe. The Eucharistic life is the Church's life. It is man's response to God's greatest gift.

(4) Finally, the thoughtful man must know that this awareness of who he is, gained most perfectly in the Eucharist, can never end in a unilateral relationship with God. He does not enter it simply, nor even primarily, to save his own soul. It is gained in the Body of Christ, the fellowship of all believers, but it does not even end here. On the Cross and in the Eucharist Jesus says, 'This is my Blood of the New Testament, which is shed for you, and for many . . .' So our real mission is to communicate His life to the many for whom He died. This is the true vocation of all Christian people.

In the Beatitudes, Christ did not say, 'Blessed are the Episcopalians, for they shall inherit the Kingdom of God.' He set an even higher standard of excellence. The world will always press us to discover a self-interest, and if we allow even the slightest impression of this to prevail, then we shall not be able to confront men effectively with the Lord Jesus Christ whom we love and serve. They can cancel easily our witness and go back to their old ways. We are interested primarily in ourselves, the maintenance of our own Christian society. They may compliment us for doing

good or for being a worthwhile institution for human better-
ment, but they will not be compelled to make a decision for
Christ.

I offer no criticism of bean suppers and bazaars, important
sometimes in the maintenance of the local congregation for
reasons both of financial return and of the fellowship of
work. But we must recognize these things for what they are
—duties performed simply to maintain the life of the family,
just as are ushering, choir singing, church-school teaching,
and money counting. One of the real disciplines of a bishop's
life is often listening to announcement periods or the reading of parish bulletins, when the impression is seemingly
given that these church maintenance tasks are major reasons
for the Church's existence. Seemingly, to an outsider, this
is the Church's mission. A noble, great, heroic calling? I
leave it to you to answer.

The Cross of Jesus Christ is a gigantic plus sign, and those
of us who are learning to pick it up must know that Christians regard the church maintenance tasks simply as duty,
for which no reward or credit is given. This applies also to
our whole stewardship. We give 10 per cent of time and
money as simply duty, to maintain the life of our family;
but the other 90 per cent also belongs to God, to be offered.
Human society makes no mistakes on this duty business.
How many of us have received a letter of thanks from the
government for paying our income tax? How many of us
know joy from so doing? The real joy of citizenship comes
when we have gone beyond the call of duty to do something for the enrichment of our community.

So it is with the Christian life, learned and lived in the
Eucharist. The glorious mission of the Church is not to make
or maintain more Episcopalians, but to relate all men to
God, to extend the life of the Lord Jesus Christ into the

world. Here is life poured out. Here is Jesus Christ, ministering to the suffering, the hungry, the friendless, the needy.
For this is the world's condition. If you have received the
Lord Jesus, you must share Him with all men regardless of
race or condition. He shines forth in you, and men see the
radiance and know that you have been with God. Their response is not up to you then. All you can know is that you
have done your part.

Sick persons and sick parishes alike are concerned only
with their own survival. This is why they know such great
unhappiness, pettiness, and bickering. They are living only
for themselves. But the supernatural power of the liturgy is
so strong that it should never fail to achieve a deep formative
influence in the people of God. The more conscious and inti-
mate is the active participation of the congregation, the
greater and richer is this influence. The sacred liturgy not
only determines external rules of action or patterns of community life, but it also creates a spirit and an interior attitude that will enable people to enter into a community with
a generous and brotherly disposition and with the capacity
to work. In this community, they will form the climate con-
genial to a human social order, based on justice and per-
meated with charity.

When we learn the language of the liturgy, with its social
implications, we feel the presence and claim of that immense community which is the Church, and of the smaller
worshipping community that actually represents the Church.
We overcome the narrow limits of individualism, tinged
sometimes with egotism, and open the gates of the Spirit
and the heart to this broader society. Then life becomes
heroic and the Christian vocation noble.

These are things the thoughtful man must know.

INDEX

Angels, 123–4
Architecture, 72
Aristotle, 13, 76, 79

Baptism, 49, 136
Benét, Stephen Vincent, 45
Bible, *see* Scriptures
Bouyer, L., 47

Calvary, *see* Passion
Calvin, John, 109
Catechumens, 47–8, 57, 63
Christian Year, 49, 60, 61
Church, 17, 20, 73, 75, 90ff., 122, 140
Confirmation, 57, 62, 136
Creation, 52, 53–5, 60, 77ff.
Cult, 27, 29, 31, 36

Democracy, 91–2, 97–8
Dix, G., 121

Eastern Church, 9, 79, 117ff.
Epiclesis, 121, 130
Eschatology, 79, 129, 130–31, 132
Ethics, 28, 30, 32, 37, 68–9, 71
Eucharist, central act of the, Church, 3–6, 45
    ethical and social implications, 37, 67ff.

instructed, 58
memorial, 8–11, 130
mysterion, 6, 105
offering, 15–16, 18–19, 36, 54, 67, 77–8, 80, 126, 129
sacrifice, 7–9, 15–19, 123, 125–7
thanksgiving, 54, 75, 77, 127–8, 140

Great Entrance, 79
Guardini, R., 53, 71

Incarnation, 13–14, 25, 38, 52, 126

Kraemer, H., 90, 92, 106, 109

Ladd, W. P., 76
Lichtenberger, A. C., 103
Liturgical Movement, 71–2, 77, 88–9, 94, 117–18, 131, 132

Man, nature of, 74–6, 101, 128
Mascall, E. L., 55–6
Meynell, Alice, 51, 55
Middle Ages, 11, 13, 48, 89, 123
Mission, 92–4, 95, 103, 110, 131, 141
Morality, *see* Ethics

145